The Cult of the Cat

with 130 illustrations, 16 in colour

Thames and Hudson

For Alexander

I am most grateful to the following, who, each in
their own way, have inspired or made possible the
writing of this book. My wife Pauline and my
daughter Roxanne; Lynx, Desmond Morris, Iris
Parker, Geoff and Pat Saunders, the staff of
Southampton University Library, Al Stewart, Keith
and Cynthia Stringfellow, Tula, and Peter Ucko.

NJS, Bognor Regis, 1990

ART AND IMAGINATION

Contents

Under the Spell of the Cat

Few symbols have endured as long, or are so widespread, as that of the feline. Ever since our species first evolved, cats have had a profound impact on the human imagination. The big cats have inspired both admiration and fear, and have been incorporated into the religious beliefs, ideologies and artistic traditions of a succession of ancient civilizations and modern peoples alike. Small cats, whether wild, or, more recently, domesticated, have similarly found a place in our superstitions and affections, as miniature representatives of the feline spirit. All have become, in one sense or another, surrounded by ritual or cult activity.

Early humans probably watched the big cats with considerable fascination and interest, for, unlike themselves, these powerful carnivores must have seemed perfectly in tune with their environment. Superb predators who hunted their prey on their own terms, they were capable of bursts of speed and feats of strength that humans could never match. Even the smaller cats could climb trees, swim, and display an agility far beyond that of humans.

What human beings could not equal was, by definition, regarded as super-human, particularly when reinforced by the nocturnal habit of these creatures, who could hunt their prey with eyes which shone like mirrors. The seemingly magical combination of individual strength, agility and night-vision contrasted strongly with the daytime activities of comparatively weaker humans, and created a singularly powerful image which was implanted into the consciousness of our early ancestors.

This image has persisted throughout history and still bewitches us today. Our own culture's obsession with cats it but the most recent manifestation of an age-old relationship between humans and felines. What we believe about cats determines our attitudes towards them, and consequently we react in distinctive ways – with fear or affection, for example – when confronted with their presence or their likeness. That past societies, too, possessed a diversity of attitudes to, and behaviour concerning, felines, is apparent from the many images, beliefs and cults which have been associated with these majestic creatures since the earliest times.

Powerful icons from the past, the varied images of the cat serve to connect their nature, as one of the earth's most successful predators, with universal human concerns. The effect of the natural animal on human imagination has produced a kaleidoscope of naturalistic, mystical and anthropomorphic images – felines have often been regarded not simply as animals, but as the conspiratorial agents of sorcery, witchcraft and supernatural powers. Undisputed masters of stealth and cunning, and, for the big cats, of strength and ferocity, felines have combined the notion of survival with the symbolism of success, and have been associated with the most powerful individuals in human societies – warriors, shamans, chiefs and, ultimately, royalty.

The rendering of the feline form in the art and mythology of ancient and more recent societies reveals that psychological and cultural factors have been at work. Apart from naturalistic depictions, such as the Lion Gate of Mycenae, the ivory leopards of Benin or the jaguars on ancient Peruvian pottery, there are the more frequent representations of strange, anthropo-morphic creatures, hybrids of the human imagination, which freely mix the feline form with that of other animals or humans themselves. From the earliest of times the feline was recognized as possessing a potential for representing particular human qualities. When depicted in the art of Pharaonic Egypt, Classical Greece or Pre-Columbian America, these qualities were shown as fantastical beings that only ever inhabited the minds of their creators.

Today, the cult of the cat is more pervasive, and complex, than ever. Although magical images of huge cat-like monsters, sorcerers, demons and deities have been banished to the realm of fantasy and film, images of the big cats are still universally employed to convey authority, power, prestige and wealth, from coats of arms to fast cars and jewelry. Countless households are the domain of a seemingly infinite variety of domesticated felines. Current ideas about cats as pets reveal much about the way we live, our mores and our ever-changing view of the natural world and our place within it, just as ancient attitudes revealed similar features of past societies. While modern attitudes would doubtless seem as strange and incompre-hensible to our ancestors as their beliefs appear to us, the image of the feline has nevertheless retained its hold over the human imagination.

Predators in the Landscape

Most human beliefs concerning cats have clustered around five distinct types of feline – lion, tiger, leopard, jaguar and, since Egyptian times, the domestic cat. Each has occupied a special place in the myths, stories, superstitions and beliefs of the peoples whose physical universe they shared. However, it is probably true that all cats, large and small, have had the potential for becoming cult objects at one time or another.

In order to appreciate the fascination which felines have exercised over humankind since earliest times, it is necessary to understand the animals themselves. Felines are the most varied and widespread of nature's predators – their form being the supreme expression of hunting design. They combine power, speed, stealth, camouflage and 'intelligence', and are the earth's most efficient predators, dominating many environments.

Their sheer diversity and specialized hunting abilities allow them to stalk and kill the same prey as humans and they are thus keen competitors, for rabbits, deer, buffalo, or other quarry. On occasion, they hunt humans themselves.

These highly specialized carnivores are the result of millions of years of evolution, with most of the forty modern types of cat having been in existence for about the past 2 million years. During the last Ice Age, at a time when humans were colonizing many parts of the world, Europe was home to oversized cave lions and leopards, China to giant tigers and America to huge jaguars. Adapted to hunting large prey, such as mammoth, elephant and giant sloth, these great predators died out as their prey mostly disappeared around 10,000 years ago.

In many ways the story of the lion (*Felis leo*) exemplifies the accomplishments of the cat family. Originating in Africa, the lion achieved its greatest size in Europe. Its remains have been found in northeast Siberia and in Chinese caves which were also occupied by early humans. The success of this super-predator was unparalleled. It ranged from desert margins to arctic steppes and grassy savannahs in Africa, Europe, Asia and the Americas. No other species of land mammal had ever conquered such an extensive and diverse area before the advent of humans.

Today, the lion is mainly restricted to Africa, particularly Kenya, Tanzania and Uganda, though a few have managed to cling on in the Gir Forest of northeast India. It survived until the Christian era in northern Greece but has, more recently, disappeared also from Iran, the Levant and North Africa. This original wider distribution is significant, for lion imagery appears in ancient times in the religion and art of those regions where the animal itself has not survived, for example in Turkey, where lion bones have been found at the site of ancient Troy.

Often referred to as the 'King of Beasts', the lion is distinguished by its social behaviour, based on the pride, and by the impressive mane of the male. Master of the veldt, it possesses both keen eyesight and co-operative hunting tactics (it has the largest brain of all the felines), which allow it to prey on wildebeest, zebra and even giraffe, by night and day. Lions are not, however, averse to taking smaller animals and will chase off or kill lesser felines such as leopards and cheetahs, and, sometimes, humans.

The leopard (*Panthera pardus*), sometimes referred to as the panther, and itself a cult animal, was found throughout most of Europe during the last Ice Age. It later spread to Asia Minor and today resides in both Asia and Africa where, in densely forested areas, 'black panthers' are common. The leopard is highly adaptable, equally at home in the Atlas Mountains of North Africa, the snowy regions of Siberia or the jungles of Vietnam and Malaysia. It climbs and swims well and its stealth makes it the most accomplished stalker of all big cats, counting among its prey gazelle, baboon, deer and, under certain circumstances, humans. The famous 'Leopard of Rudaprayag' terrorized the Garhwal region of India for nine years, killing at least 125 people until it was shot in 1926. Its uncanny ability to avoid its hunters for so long led the local inhabitants to brand it a were-leopard – a half-human, half-animal being.

In India and Asia it is the Tiger (*Panthera tigris*) which dominates the feline family. Evidence suggests that the tiger originated in Siberia, subsequently moving south to China, Malaya and India. Powerfully built, tigers take readily to water and on occasion climb trees. They are known also to wander over wide areas, often covering tens of miles over a period of several weeks. The tiger ranges from the Siberian steppes to tropical rainforests and exhibits a wide variety of colouration and markings. No black specimen has ever been verified but white tigers are well known. By and large they are solitary hunters and though many reports have stressed their man-eating habits, such behaviour is usually due to special local conditions, such as drought, famine or the encroachment of human villages on forest areas. The Siberian tiger is the largest of the big cats to have survived to the present day.

In the Americas, where there have been no lions, tigers or leopards since the last Ice Age, it is the agile Puma (*Felis concolour*) and the larger, more powerful, Jaguar (*Panthera onca*) which represent the big cats. Pumas feature only occasionally in religious beliefs, but the visually dramatic jaguar is frequently represented. The jaguar probably had a Eurasian origin: ancestral jaguars survived there until about half a million years ago. In the Americas, jaguars which were considerably larger than today's had appeared by about 2 million years ago, and were the most common feline predator, with the exception of the sabre-toothed cat.

The domestic cat first appeared during the Egypt of the New Kingdom, around 1500 BC, though an earlier date cannot be ruled out. The exact course of events which led to domestication remains unclear, but most experts agree that early domesticated varieties descended either from the African Wild Cat (*Felis silvestris libyca*) or from interbreeding between this and the larger Jungle Cat (*Felis chaus*), perhaps in temple precincts or around human habitation. Whatever its exact origin, the domestic cat is now the most successful and widespread member of the cat family, increasing in numbers at a time when, for a variety of reasons, many of the big cats are facing extinction.

Of Humans and Felines

The impact of predatory felines in the landscape and their effect on surrounding prey must have made as strong an impression on early humans as they did on later tribal peoples. Throughout human history the deadly nature and beauty of these supreme hunters had been a source of fear, respect, emulation and competition for societies firmly locked into a hunting, and, on occasion, scavenging ethos. That such vital concerns as success in hunting and individual safety were both directly and indirectly affected by the activities of the hunting cats suggests that early confrontations, during the 3 million years of the Old Stone Age, may well have been the source for all subsequent cultic activity associated with these cats and their smaller cousins.

Recent investigations in Africa into the remains of the world's earliest humans indicate that such relationships between humans and felines stretch back deep into prehistoric times. Shattered human bone remains, dated to around 1.5 million years ago, were originally thought to prove that the early form of human known as *Australopithecus* was a mighty hunter. This traditional view has been challenged by recent work, which has suggested that perhaps the big cats played a previously unsuspected role.

Studies of the hunting and eating habits of modern leopards show that they drag the carcasses of their prey into the nearest tree to devour them in safety. On the waterless landscape of the African veldt, trees cluster around fissures in the ground, which not only give access to underground water, but also provide natural lairs for the hunting cats. On comparing the typical bone damage from such modern activity with the ancient bones found at some of these early human sites, and assuming that ancient leopards acted similarly to their modern counterparts, it was concluded that skull fractures and bone damage were probably the result of leopard attack rather than human assault. On some occasions at least, *Australopithecus* may have been the hunted rather than the hunter.

Formative experiences at this remote time were reinforced over subsequent millennia, when the idea of supernatural cats, or the notion of human transformation into felines, developed. By around 38,000 years ago, there is evidence for both naturalistically rendered felines and composite human-feline creatures.

Naturalistic felines were represented in the explosion of Western European cave art which occurred at this time. Caves themselves, of course, had always been preferred shelters for the big cats, and had already become important as places of cultic activity for humans. The depiction of animals in Palaeolithic cave art tended to favour the horse, bison and other herbivores, with carnivores being comparatively rare. However, where predators did appear, the principal one shown was the cave lion, usually identified by its canines and muzzle, depicted in profile, though none of those so far discovered has exhibited a full mane. Indeed, felines are often the most inaccurately portrayed of all Palaeolithic figures, particularly when it came to rendering their dangerous fangs. This may have been due to the risks incurred in observing them close up.

Detailed studies of this artistic tradition have revealed that the lion, along with other carnivores such as the bear, were usually found at the back of a cave, separated from herbivorous animals – perhaps reflecting ancient beliefs which required that natural and supernatural hunters should be kept at a respectful distance from their prey. At the famous French cave sites of

Les Trois Frères, the lions' bodies were engraved in profile, but the heads, with their large round eyes, stare at the viewer face on. At Lascaux, a group of seven lions appear in what has been called the 'Chambre des Félins'. In the centre of the scene, two large lions confront each other face to face, perhaps fighting for the right to kill or eat the bisons and horses which surround them. The artistic treatment of felines in cave art varied from place to place and a particularly abstract lion, or perhaps leopard, is depicted at the cave of La Baume-Latrone, rearing threateningly over a much smaller mammoth.

More mysterious, perhaps mythical, images have also been found. Some 32,000 years ago a Stone Age sculptor made a beautiful and rare mammoth-ivory carving of a lion-headed anthropomorphic being, nearly a foot tall. This extraordinary work indicates how very early on human beings were thinking about, and producing, objects which symbolized rather than reflected the natural world – objects that perhaps represented ideas about the potential metamorphosis of humans and animals.

In the Americas, where there are neither cave paintings nor bone carvings to record the ancient relationship between humans and big cats, confrontations must nevertheless have been frequent. In cave shelters, the remains of Ice Age jaguars and humans have been found, and from California, sabre-toothed cat bones have preserved what have been interpreted as the deliberate marks of human use. As elsewhere, the large native American cats would have been major competitors to humans, and were similarly attracted to ancient water holes, where their remains have been found in huge numbers.

There can be little doubt that during the long march to civilization humans and felines came into violent conflict. On some occasions, felines would frighten the prey animals and so disrupt human hunting activities; on other occasions, humans may have learned how to scavenge a lion's kill, perhaps even making a precarious living from it. Whether competing for food, water or cave shelter, humans have had a close relationship with cats for untold millennia, and it is perhaps no surprise that the predatory feline should feature so prominently in the metaphysical worlds which surviving hunter-gatherer societies have created, and the art and mythology which characterize them.

Hunters of the Spirit Realm

In a world without agriculture or science, where the activities of spirits and the power of sorcery were regarded as real, large and small cats possessed that magical aura which made them feared nocturnal predators, not just in the physical world, but in the supernatural realm as well.

Those societies scattered around the world which today still maintain this way of life also retain vestiges of age-old beliefs, telling of fearsome half-human, half-feline creatures that stalk the realm of ancestors and spirits, and hunt the souls of unwary travellers. These supernatural beings cross the boundary between life and death with impunity and are often regarded as the spirits of evil sorcerers or even the transformed essence of shamans.

In the hunt or at war, where chance and skill played an equally vital role, human cultures wove a rich and distinctive tapestry of myth and belief around real and imagined events. Such beliefs bound men and women more closely to their environment, increased their chances of survival and made metaphysical sense of the world around them. The identification of hunters, warriors and shamans with lions, tigers or jaguars was a means of acquiring 'prestige by association'; the power of nature was tamed for social and cultural ends.

The hunting and gathering way of life, where collective survival depended on individual success, was based on an intimate understanding of the environment, its wildlife, and other human societies. There was much for humans to observe and imitate in the appearance and behaviour of felines – knowledge that could be used when hunting animals for food or other humans in war. Fierce Amazonian warriors were often referred to as 'jaguars', the Dayaks of Sarawak went into battle wearing pelts of the Clouded Leopard, and the tall spearmen of the East African Maasai wore impressive lion manes.

In small and transient societies, the only recognized social role is usually that of the sorcerer or shaman, who maintains a special relationship with the all-powerful animal and ancestor spirits of the forest. Unlike a magician or a mystic, the shaman is a true master of spirits, controlling their activities for the benefit of the tribe. To reinforce his power, the shaman often identified himself with the feline – the dominant hunter and 'master of animals'. Just as the lion, leopard or jaguar were believed to control the lesser animals which were their prey, so the shaman imposed his will on other-worldly beings by 'becoming' a spirit-feline: the supernatural warrior, and the hunter and master of souls. Shamans of the North American Prairie Potawatomi believed in an Underwater Panther, called Nampe'shiu or Nampeshi'k, who inhabited the third tier of the underworld, and had a particular relationship with warriors. Their myths celebrated this great horned feline, which appeared to men who were destined to become great warriors.

The identification of felines with shamans as supernatural warriors is part of a whole system of beliefs concerning human-animal transformation – a process which produced startling cultic images in which the shapes and qualities of humans and animals are blended. From many parts of the world come stories of shamans who changed into supernatural felines – were-tigers, -leopards or -jaguars – in order to conduct their spirit-world activities.

Among the Batek Negritos, a hunting and gathering people of Malaysia, there is a rich body of belief concerning tigers, both real and supernatural. The Batek believe that at the centre of their world is a great stone pillar, at whose base many tigers live in caves. This is the home of 'Raja Yah', the king of tigers. This sacred place has a parallel in the mythical home of tigers where tiger-men are ruled over by a chief called the 'Tiger Devil' who enters the bodies of sorcerers when they invoke the tiger spirit. The inhabitants of this mythical realm look like real tigers when they are in their own village but after swimming through a special pool they emerge in human form. These supernatural tigers possessed mortal bodies, but the immortal shadow-souls of dead shamans. They were regarded as beneficent, acting as guardians of Batek society and as the teachers and spirit-helpers of Batek shamans.

Those Batek who wished to become shamans had first to learn magical songs and spells in order to acquire supernatural power. It was the spirit-tigers who possessed and dispensed the most powerful of these charms and so it was they who had to be contacted. A nervous would-be shaman had to stand guard over the fresh grave of a newly deceased person until the spirit of the dead individual appeared to him in the shape of a tiger. The novice had to control his fear, beckon the supernatural creature forward and blow smoke over it, whereupon the spirit-tiger passed on his songs and incantations of enchantment, and revealed the secrets of sending the soul on cosmic journeys through time and space.

The Batek, then, believed that shamans and tigers were associated both before and after death and that their shamans were descended from 'Raja Yah', the original tiger. When summoned, Raja Yah's spirit took control of the shaman's shadow-soul, and caused him to growl like his master. In Batek belief, the tiger-body of the shaman was similar to that of a natural tiger, and at night, when the human body of the shaman was asleep, his shadow-soul went to the tiger, but by the morning it had returned to the human body, and the tiger had gone to sleep somewhere deep in the forest.

In his tiger guise the Batek shaman roamed the forest, eavesdropping on conversations around camp fires. By harnessing the power and speed of the tiger, the shaman was believed to transform into a fierce and dangerous supernatural warrior, who patrolled the boundaries of his society and protected the cosmic identity of his group. In this way the essence of nature's most feared and successful predator was turned to the benefit of humankind.

Fierce supernatural felines also prowled the spirit worlds of many of the surviving tribes of South America. Here, the largest feline and dominant predator of the vast expanse of Amazon rainforest was the jaguar, a creature with whom hunters, warriors and shamans maintained an intimate association. In Brazil, adult men of some tribes had a jaguar tattooed on their forearms, while others prepared for war by painting themselves with black spots and making war cries which sounded like the jaguar's roar. Among some of these societies, those who had confronted and killed a jaguar gained prestige and were regarded by their enemies as being possessed of jaguar-souls, which made them fierce and doughty warriors.

Throughout the rainforest, despite its many cultures and languages, the shaman-jaguar concept was widespread and was the most enduring aspect of the mystical relationship between humans and felines. Those who encountered a jaguar in the jungle could never be sure whether it was an ordinary animal or a transformed shaman engaged in magical activities. The symbolism associated with shape-shifting reflected the spiritual link between animal and human, cat and shaman. The most powerful and dangerous human and his animal counterpart often shared the same name, for in many lowland South American societies the term 'yai' meant predator, and was applied equally to the jaguar as hunter of prey and to the shaman as killer of souls.

In eastern Bolivia, the Mojo Indians were recorded by the Jesuits as having a 'jaguar cult', where men who had survived a jaguar attack became members of a special group of shamans. They would emerge from their huts after having 'talked' with the jaguar spirit, bleeding and with clothes torn, as if they had been savaged by the cat, and demand payment of food and beer from the villagers in return for their protective services.

An Amazonian shaman could transform into a deadly spirit-jaguar by smoking strong tobacco, sniffing powerful hallucinogenic powders, or drinking narcotic beverages. Often taken during extended nocturnal rituals, accompanied by dancing, music and rhythmic chanting, these mind-altering substances allowed him to enter the dreamworld of trance, the realm of animal and ancestor spirits. The hallucinogenic agent itself was sometimes referred to as the jaguar's drug or the jaguar's sperm, and was sometimes kept in a hollow jaguar bone.

Under the influence of narcotics the Amazonian shaman saw with 'jaguar eyes': he perceived the world not as a human being but as a hunting cat, and he confronted the powers of nature on equal terms. The complex anthropomorphic imagery of man-jaguar transformation has been explored for many years by the Colombian anthropologist, Gerardo Reichel-Dolmatoff:

How like a jaguar does a man become? A payé-turned-jaguar is, for all exterior purposes, a true jaguar: he has the voice of a jaguar, he devours raw meat, he sleeps on the ground, and he has the highly developed vision and olfactory sense of the feline. . . . But in one aspect he is not a jaguar at all: in his attitude toward human beings. In this, he does not behave like a jaguar, but like a man – a man devoid of all cultural restrictions, but still a man. The motivation of revenge and the acts of sexual assault, of attacking from behind and in a pack, and of severing the victim's head are not jaguar but human traits. What turns jaguar, then, is that part of man's personality that resists and rejects cultural conventions. The jaguar of the hallucinatory sphere, the jaguar-monster of Tukano tales, is a man's alter ego, now roaming free and untrammeled, and acting out his deepest desires and fears. (Reichel-Dolmatoff 1975: 132)

The jaguar symbolism employed by Amazonian shamans was in part an acknowledgment that of all jungle creatures it was the jaguar which consistently threatened human survival, stalking by night the same animals that humans hunt by day. The jaguar, with its naturally mirrored eyes which pierced the gloom of night, was regarded as the 'Master of Animals'.

Symbols of Royalty and Power

For centuries, hunters, warriors, shamans and sorcerers of hunting societies the world over associated themselves with the big cats. The significance of such identification went far beyond a desire for success in battle or beliefs about supernatural spirit-felines; the cult of the cat penetrated deeply into the nature of politics and, for many cultures, into the symbolism and patronage of royal dynasties.

The close relationship between felines and royalty can be traced throughout human history. Solomon's throne was supported by lions, and in ancient Egypt, where the coronation of a new pharaoh found the ruler sitting on the 'Lion Throne', the sphinx was a personification of royalty, blending the body of a lion with the head of a pharaoh in a vivid representation of a half-human, half-feline creature. The sphinx was believed to be the 'Protector of Thresholds', who would seize those who violated the sanctity of holy places.

In prehistoric Mesopotamia and surrounding regions, the lion had been identified with royal status since the earliest of times – a close relationship which was reflected in art, architecture and the new practice of writing. An inscribed stone tablet of an early king was discovered held between the paws of a bronze lion, and at Babylon three great male lions decorated the glazed-brick facade of Nebuchadnezzar's throne room. The early Sumerian book of Gilgamesh celebrated the many adventures of this archetypal hero figure, who was said to have been the founder of kingship throughout the region. The relationship between kingship and lion symbolism permeated the region's artistic traditions. On large stone statues and small cylinder seals, Gilgamesh was portrayed clasping a lion, standing over its body, or engaged in an epic struggle with the king of beasts. Such 'contest scenes' between heroes and lions were especially popular in Mesopotamia, where successive kings had themselves portrayed in this fashion for several thousand years.

Mythological struggles between heroes and lions were also imitated in real life, as the hunting of big cats became a status activity reserved to the king and members of the royal family. The Egyptian pharaoh Amenophis III killed no fewer than 102 lions during the first ten years of his reign, and, in an unusual variation, Ramesses II went into battle accompanied by a lion. The great 7th-century BC Assyrian ruler Assurbanipal was shown confronting the beast in several reliefs discovered in his palace at the ancient city of Nineveh, and described his lion hunting thus:

> . . . lions have bred in mighty numbers. Through the killing of cattle, small stock and man they have become bold. The mountain shakes with the thunder of their roars, the game of the plains has fled. They constantly kill the livestock of the fields and they spill the blood of men and cattle. The herdsmen and the supervisors are weeping; the families are mourning. The misdeeds of these lions have been reported to me. In the course of my expedition I have penetrated their hiding places and destroyed their lairs. For my regal amusement I have caught the Desert King by his tail, and on the instructions of my helpers, the Gods Nusib and Nergal, I have split his head with my two-handed sword. (Guggisberg 1961: 293)

The relationship between the big cats and royalty was also clearly seen in later Hellenistic times, when it symbolized the aggressiveness and majesty of powerful Macedonian kings who had brought to an end the Classical Greek tradition of democracy. Alexander the Great, in his role as 'World Conqueror', identified himself with the figure of Heracles, and was often depicted on coins and marble sculpture wearing a lion's-head helmet. After his death, the struggle for succession led to huge festivals and games being arranged by the contenders, at which the royal felines – lions, leopards and tigers – were displayed in ever increasing numbers. The appearance of the still exotic tiger, and the large number of lions and leopards which were put on show, indicated that each of the would-be successors controlled that part of Alexander's empire which was the animal's natural home, and so had a legitimate claim.

The spectacular display of large numbers of big cats was one of the traditions which the Romans inherited from the Hellenistic world. In 55 BC Pompey showed and then had slaughtered 600 lions and 410 leopards as well as a huge number of other animals, and, later, lions were set against each other, and against tigers, leopards, and humans – a form of 'entertainment' which ended with the lion-Christian confrontations of the later Roman empire. It is a sad fact that the popularity of such mass public slaughter among the Romans probably led to the disappearance of the lion and leopard throughout the Mediterranean area by the 2nd century AD. Here, at least, the ancient association of kings with big cats led, through a strange course of events, to the virtual elimination of the animals themselves.

The Roman attitude to the big cats revealed that the acquisition, humiliation and public death of these magnificent beasts was itself a metaphor for imperial conquest and domination. Some two thousand years later, similar attitudes characterized the hunting and trophy taking activities of British empire builders. As Harriet Ritvo says in her book, *The Animal Estate*, the subjugation of nature's fiercest and most dangerous predators was a metaphorical statement for the conquest of foreign peoples and exotic lands by the British.

Large numbers of lions, tigers and leopards were transported from the far reaches of empire to be exhibited, suitably caged, in Victorian zoos for the entertainment and enlightenment of the masses. This statement of military power and political influence was paralleled by a popular literary genre, which praised the courage and ingenuity of the White Hunter who overcame his 'treacherous' foe to bring back vast quantities of skins and stuffed heads as trophies both to British manhood and imperial success. Such events are an indication of how ambiguous social attitudes towards the big cats have led to their mass slaughter, whether for entertainment of the Roman masses, the patriotic fervour of British empire builders, or their modern equivalent, the luxury fur trade.

In Pre-Columbian America, ancient Maya dynasts and nobles adopted the hieroglyphic sign for 'jaguar' in their official titles, and we find such names as 'Shield Jaguar', 'Lord Jaguar' and 'Bird Jaguar' referred to in Maya inscriptions. Maya rulers were often shown seated on thrones carved in the shape, or draped with the pelt, of the jaguar, and at the famous site of Chichen-Itza in Mexico the renowned 'Red Jaguar Throne' is rendered as a life-size jaguar and decorated with some 73 jade discs. Jaguar apparel was also reserved for the elite: an elaborately dressed ruler in a jaguar skin suit is shown carved in wood at Tikal in Guatemala. Important individuals, presumably princes and kings, were interred with jaguar pelts, claws and skulls.

Aztec Mexico was the scene of one of the most dramatic manifestations of the relationship of cat and king. Here, where the jaguar had been the centre of religious beliefs for centuries, the 16th-century Spanish chronicler, Sahagún, referred to it as the 'Lord of Animals', noble and princely, cautious, wise and proud. Identified with Aztec sorcerers, who dressed in jaguar skin as they went about their evil works, and with the elite 'Jaguar Warrior Society', America's most powerful cat was also believed to be the most potent aspect of Tezcatlipoca, the all-seeing, all-powerful 'Lord of the Smoking Mirror', patron deity of Aztec royalty.

The accession to power of a new emperor was drenched in jaguar symbolism, associating the new king with age-old shamanistic beliefs concerning supernatural power, and, by analogy, linking the all-seeing qualities of jaguar eyes with Tezcatlipoca's magical mirror with which he saw into the very hearts of men. At his coronation, a new emperor mounted a throne decorated with jaguar skins and would ritually draw his own blood with a jaguar bone. Afterwards he was regarded as the image of the god Tezcatlipoca, whose fangs and claws he was now believed to possess.

Ancient Mexican beliefs concerning the power of the jaguar as a symbol of royalty and fertility, intimately associated with blood sacrifice, find an echo today in some of the more remote parts of Mexico. In many rural villages, the jaguar, commonly known as *tigre*, is a favourite motif for mask-makers, and there still exist springtime festivities which honour the jaguar deity. Some villages hold jaguar-dances, where young men dress as jaguars, dance, and have mock fights in the town square to encourage fertility and protect the crops. Some places have preserved a purer tradition which involves the spilling of human blood. At one village in particular, the young men wear jaguar suits, 'boxing gloves', toughened leather helmets painted with a snarling jaguar face, and a tail-like length of rope coiled around the waist. After making a three-hour trek to the summit of a local mountain, the contestants engage in dramatic fist fights whose purpose is to spill human blood in honour of the jaguar god. He is expected to acknowledge these offerings by sending rain to fertilize the maize and so provide the community with food for another year.

As in Mexico, echoes of ancient feline symbolism have lingered on in the Andes of South America, where they are related to sorcery and fertility. Among the Quechua Indians of Peru, a belief persists in a fierce winged mountain-cat called the Ccoa, which can throw lightning bolts from its luminous eyes. A most active and feared spirit, the ccoa is believed to control the weather and thus animal and crop fertility by roaring like thunder and urinating rain. It is said that there are two kinds of people, those who serve the ccoa, making it suitable offerings, and whose fields are never damaged by frost or hail, and those who are against it, who often fall ill and whose fields yield poorly. The ccoa, perhaps not surprisingly, also endows sorcerers with their supernatural power.

In ancient times it was the puma that served as the symbol of Inca royalty. After defeating his bitterest enemies, the great ruler Yupanqui, founder of the Inca empire, was glorified as a puma. In the ceremony whereby noble Inca youths were admitted into manhood, the festivities were accompanied by men wearing puma skins, who played drums of the same material. The emblems of royal adulthood included puma heads complete with golden earspools.

In more recent historical times, in the West African state of Benin, it was the privilege of kings to keep leopards, whose royal form was cast in bronze and endowed sacred status on the king's altars. The wearing of leopard skins and the holding of leopard cubs were further symbols of Benin royalty. While leopard imagery was prevalent throughout this region, it was the artisans of Benin under the patronage of their kings who produced the most numerous and varied types of bronze leopard representations, often life-size.

A dramatic but rarely reported case of big cat symbolism, which displayed the power and authority of those who used it, involved what are known as the Tibetan Tiger Rugs. During the 7th century, the Tibetan throne was covered with tiger skin, and court officials wore clothing embroidered with tiger designs and had a tiger painted on their graves.

The big cats and their skins also figured prominently in later Buddhist paintings and literature. They are particularly common in Tibetan paintings which showed the ascetic Yogins engaged in contemplation, sitting on tiger skins which were believed to protect them from all earthly disturbances. This protective aspect was also apparent in the tiger rugs that were placed at each side of the entrance to the Dalai Lama's throne room at Lhasa. Such ancient shamanistic symbolism, associating secular and spiritual leaders with carnivorous felines, is also shared by the Hindu religion, where the skins of both the tiger and the leopard were considered sacred symbols of Shiva, the deity particularly associated with yoga. For Buddhists and Hindus alike, to sit on a tiger skin or rug symbolized the individual's control over tiger-spirits, that is, powerful desires.

The use of feline names in the titles of chiefs, kings and emperors was a widespread phenomenon. Haile Selassie, the last of a long line of Ethiopian emperors, was given the title 'King of Kings of Ethiopia, Lion of Judah, the Elect of God', and for royalty, as for sorcerers, the individual gained prestige and power by association with both the strength of the real cat and the supernatural abilities of its spirit form. The feline was often the dominant icon of royalty. In West Africa, for instance, the Mali empire was founded by Mari-Jata, the Lion of Mali. Similarly, the founder of the royal lineage in Dahomey was said to have been born of the union of a princess and a leopard. A Swahili chronicle preserves a tradition whereby a lion is said to roar when a ruler is born, and among the Ambo of Zambia, a chief was thought to change into a lion at the moment of death.

One of the clearest examples of the relationship between felines, royalty and politics was found among the Banyang peoples of southeastern Nigeria and western Cameroun. According to the anthropologist Malcolm Ruel, order and stability in this society could be described as the politics of leopard-giving, for when a leopard was killed it was given by the hunter to his superior, who in turn passed it up the hierarchy until it reached the village leader. The chief then 'appeased' the dead animal and, after having skinned it, divided the meat for consumption by the village's group of leading men, who were often referred to as 'leopard people' or the 'leopard association'. The ritual of giving a leopard was – where the animal itself symbolized male power – a focal point for the display of constitutional politics.

A similar link between felines and politics could be found in the Luapala valley, which divided Zambia and Zaire. Elaborate purification rites had to be performed if a lion was killed; failure to perform these rites was believed to bring about 'a plague of lions' and drive the local ruler to insanity. The rites reasserted the political order by requiring that representatives of each political level, culminating with the king, stepped on the lion's skin. In this way the monarch re-established his 'dominion over lions', the lions here being metaphors for rival headmen and chiefs.

Where African felines have been such potent images for so many centuries, it is not surprising that more mysterious ancient traditions and beliefs have also survived. Magic charms made of a lion's paw are believed to protect against enemy attack. Lion fat is thought to cure a variety of illnesses, and, when rubbed into the skin, to engender strength and courage. Bezoar stones, which form in the lion's stomach, are regarded as powerful amulets against attack by wild animals, and the lion's heart is particularly valued as a symbol of power. Belief in the 'were-lion', a dangerous half-human, half-lion creature, is one of the most enduring traditions. In some parts of East Africa were-lions are thought to be witches in lion shape, and in other regions all man-eating lions are believed to be sorcerers in disguise.

A particularly violent and bloody cult, which linked witchcraft, ritual murder and lion symbolism, evolved in the early part of the 20th century in Africa. At Singida in central Tanzania, local sorcerers bought or stole mentally handicapped boys and kept them isolated from the outside world until they had grown up. They were then dressed in lion skins and hired out by their owners as professional assassins.

Known as 'Lion Men', they came to public attention in 1920, when a British colonial government official reported that some 200 people had lost their lives near Singida. At first, man-eating lions were suspected, but the authorities soon realized that the murders had been committed by lion men, working on behalf of witch-doctors who were extorting money from the local population. One example, among many hundreds, tells of three people who were sentenced to death in 1957 for their part in the murder of a five-year-old girl; they were accused of having used a lion man to kill the child, who had been torn from her mother's arms and carried off into the bush, where her scattered remains were later discovered. Similar stories come from West Africa, where the leopard, long a cult animal of royalty, was employed as a symbol of fear by 'Leopard Men Societies' who terrorized rural villages well into the present century. Dressed in leopard skins, often wearing wooden sandals which left paw prints, and wielding iron prongs, they disfigured their victims to imitate an attack by the big cat.

The Cat in Iconography and Religion

The cultic association of cats and humans, whether as spirit-familiars of shamans, patrons of royalty, or guardians of heroes and the dead, was dramatically reflected in the symbols and imagery which permeated religion and art. From the dawn of civilized life in the farming villages of prehistoric Turkey, to the early civilizations of Mesopotamia, Egypt, China and the Americas, come startlingly powerful images of cats, large and small, naturalistic and fantastical, but always imposing and mysterious – an icon of power and an object of religious cult.

After their first appearance in the cave paintings of the European Stone Age, cats retained their fascination for later and more sophisticated societies. Carved in stone, modelled in clay and painted in brilliant coloured murals, feline images, particularly of the big cats, were found adorning many examples of ancient architecture. One of the earliest was the Neolithic village of Catal Hüyük in southern Turkey, which flourished around 6,000 BC. Here, preserved in a small shrine, a beautifully modelled and painted relief showed two colourful leopards confronting each other. Figurines discovered at the site portrayed what have been called supernatural beings riding leopards, holding leopard cubs, or sitting on leopard-shaped thrones.

Whether these leopards were deities in their own right or the spirit-helpers of a female fertility goddess remains a mystery, but the modelled leopards found in the shrine had a parallel some 3,000 years later in Mesopotamia. A unique mural shows two large leopards, painted in red and black, as guardian figures on the altar decoration of a sanctuary. This protective aspect of the leopard was evidently shared by the other big cat of the region, as shown by the two terracotta lions which stood guard over the temple gateways at the ancient city of Shaduppum, and two bronze examples, complete with inlaid eyes, which watched vigilantly over another ancient sanctuary at Mari.

Perhaps the most famous example of this aspect of feline symbolism comes from the great city of Babylon, where the lion was a symbol of Ishtar, the goddess of war. In the imposing Processional Way, which led to Babylon's Ishtar Gate, high defensive walls were decorated with some 120 lions in glazed-brick relief, with white bodies and yellow manes set against a blue background. This imposing display could not have failed to impress all who made their way along the great approach to the ancient city. The image of the big cats as symbolic protectors was also popular further north, where great stone lions protected the monumental entrances to Hittite fortresses, and, similarly, on the western side of the Aegean, where the famous Bronze Age city of Mycenae had its own spectacular Lion Gate.

Ancient Egypt, in its art and hieroglyphic inscriptions, has preserved a unique and well documented manifestation of beliefs concerned with cat worship. Cult activities, reflecting the Egyptian fascination with felines, focussed on two anthropomorphic deities, the lion-headed goddess Sekhmet and her sister, the cat-headed Bastet. These two were regarded as the all-seeing eyes of the sun god Ra, an indication perhaps that the keen vision of felines was acknowledged and put to appropriate mythological use. Sekhmet's association with the 'King of Beasts' is not uncommon, but that of Bastet, based on smaller, initially wild, and ultimately domesticated cats, was unique.

Lions were particularly significant in Egyptian cosmology and that of its successor, the Nubian kingdom of Kush, where Apedamak, their supreme deity, was represented as a lion-headed being. At the temple of Ra at Heliopolis, a lion cult was practiced, whose priests affected great solicitude for the big cats, decreeing public mourning at the death of one of these sacred animals.

Cult centres to Sekhmet were often located at the mouths of desert wadis, the boundary between the safety of the irrigated and civilized Nile valley and the untamed desert, the natural abode of the predatory lion. Hieroglyphic inscriptions refer to the lioness as 'the great one', the mistress of the desert, and note the sharp eyes and pointed claws with which she hunted her prey at night. Sekhmet's association with the lion's strength and Ra's power came together in the description of her as the destroyer of the sun god's enemies, and she was often depicted in imposing stone sculptures, wearing the solar disc of Ra as a prominent part of her striking headdress.

By the time of the New Kingdom dynasties, cult worship had focussed also around the more benign Bastet. In artistic representations, Bastet displayed the greatest variation of all Egyptian goddesses. Originating, like Isis, in the Nile delta region, she too was considered a daughter of Ra, and, as the Lady of Life, expressed fertility and maternity, but possessed also a mysterious link with the shadowy world of the dead. Indeed, the first appearance of this unique creature was on an early papyrus where she was seen participating in funerary rituals. Bastet's relationship with Ra, as one of his all-seeing eyes, was illustrated by the Egyptian name for cat, *mau*, which means 'to see', and representations of her often display the *utchat* or sacred eye motif. The combination of the feline form with the *utchat* design was thought to have been especially powerful as a talisman against evil, particularly if the amulet was engraved with the name of Bastet.

The goddess is mainly known from the many different types of bronze statuettes that have survived: long- and short-eared varieties, human-limbed, cat-limbed and cat-tailed types are all known. Throughout the Egyptian pantheon, only the figure of Bastet varies in this way, indicative perhaps of age-old beliefs in the transformational potential of the feline. An implement often carried by Bastet linked the magical qualities of felines with sorcery and divination – the so-called sistrum or magic rattle, used by women to repel evil spirits.

The cult centre for Bastet's worship was the sacred city of Bubastis, east of the Nile delta. It contained what the Greek historian Herodotus regarded as Egypt's most beautiful temple. Approached by an impressively wide road, it had the appearance of an island because it was surrounded by broad canals fed by the Nile. Built from blocks of red granite, the central shrine contained the cult image of the goddess, and was encircled by a grove of tall trees. Inside, various scenes and hieroglyphic inscriptions honoured Bastet. There were also regular holidays in her honour, and an annual festival, for which her statue was brought from its enclosure and transported by river barge along the Nile. Herodotus describes the long journeys people made in order to participate in this festival. Every year, around springtime, thousands of devotees left their homes and travelled along the Nile, singing, dancing and drinking until they reached Bubastis, where, after more wine was consumed, many sacrifices were made. The immense popularity of Bastet survived well into the Christian era, disappearing only in AD 392, when the Christian emperor Theodosius outlawed all forms of paganism.

The special veneration accorded to Bastet extended to domestic cats, which were regarded as the living form of the goddess. The social and cultural background against which the domestic cat first appeared was greatly different from today's. Ancient Egyptians, like today's cat-owners, were particularly fond of their pets and treated them with the utmost care and attention. However, it is difficult to judge how much this behaviour was influenced by the cultic associations between cats and the goddess Bastet, who bestowed the gifts of life and fertility. Adorning their cats with silver chains, jewelled collars and golden ear-rings may have been not so much an act of affection as of reverence, and so only partly analogous to similar modern habits.

The attention which the Egyptians lavished on their cats was particularly evident in the reverential treatment of their dead pets. When a cat died, the household entered a period of mourning and lamentation, which included shaving off the eyebrows – perhaps a link with the eye symbolism of Bastet. The cat's body was conveyed to a specialist embalmer, and, after being treated with aromatic oils and swathed in linen, it was encased in an outer binding of cloth, papier-mâché or a small wooden coffin, according to the family's means. This process completed, the cat mummy was taken for burial in one of the many cat cemeteries which dotted the banks of the Nile, or, perhaps, to the largest and most sacred cemetery of all, at Bubastis. The number of cats which received such elaborate treatment was enormous, as the excavation of a cat cemetery at Beni Hassan in 1889 showed – from this site alone some 300,000 mummified cats were recovered. Somewhat mysteriously, though many other animals were similarly treated, only in cat mummies were human bones shaped and substituted for feline remains.

During Classical Greek and Hellenistic times, feline imagery is found in a variety of mythic and artistic traditions. Greek mythology harbours a wealth of symbolism concerning the lion and, to a lesser extent, the leopard. Their importance is reflected in the variety of forms in which they are represented, from naturalistic marble sculptures, frescoes and mosaics of human-feline confrontation, to fabulous monsters – joint creations of the Greek mind and inherited Near Eastern influences.

The myth of Heracles firmly established the link between the strength and prowess of lions, and brave – and often royal – individuals who, as a mark of divine favour, ultimately vanquished both their feline and human enemies. Heracles' first superhuman task was to kill the great Nemean lion, which had been sent by Hera, queen of the gods, to terrorize the ancient city of Argos. (Lions still survived in Greece in Classical times, and posed a serious threat to herds of cattle and sheep.) Heracles, finding his weapons useless against the creature's impenetrable hide, wrestled with it and finally squeezed it to death. Having skinned the huge cat with its own razor-sharp claws, Heracles wore its pelt ever after as a symbol of his prowess. The man, albeit with divine help, had assumed the lion's mantle, in both appearance and strength. This particular story, perhaps nothing other than a Greek version of the ancient Sumerian 'contest scenes' already described, nevertheless became a favourite throughout the ancient world, and is depicted in a variety of artistic media.

Commemorating his epic victory, Heracles set up a memorial at Thebes in front of the temple to Artemis, the lone huntress, who had dominion over all wild beasts including those expert hunters, the lion and the leopard. By association, Artemis was regarded as a lioness among the Olympian gods, with the figure of the beast as her image. It is probable that lions were kept in some of her forest grove sanctuaries.

Artemis' feline associations extended to Dionysus, the god of wine, revelry and nature's darker side, whose cult animal was the leopard. Dionysus was believed to have worn the leopard's skin during his sojourn in Asia, and, in a pebble mosaic from the Macedonian capital of Pella, the god was shown on leopard-back. This theme was repeated many times in antiquity, but perhaps most dramatically in a mosaic on the floor of the House of Masks on the Cycladic island of Delos, around 100 BC. An echo of this fascination with the colourful leopard, its associations with hunting, bacchic revelry, and more than a hint of eroticism, has survived intact since Greek times, through the Middle Ages, to the present. Depicted in art as an attribute of female sexuality, whether as a pelt draped in a lady's boudoir, or as a feline companion to an elegantly dressed woman, and held by a golden chain, the leopard has recently reappeared as a favourite motif in the expensive 'panther jewelry' of the 20th century. Cartier's exhibit at the 1925 Exposition des Arts Décoratifs in Paris was adorned with panther skins and wrought-iron prowling panthers, especially for the occasion. In 1948, the world's best dressed woman, in the shape of the Duchess of Windsor, commissioned the first of three pieces of her famous Cartier panther jewelry. The image of the leopard, its lithe body and visually stunning appearance, was a source of inspiration for artisans across the centuries.

Returning to Classical Greece, the symbol of the lion was also associated with water, fertility and the realm of the dead – a complex relationship, but one found in many other parts of the world. It has been suggested that lion-skin-wearing priests who performed vegetation rites were practising a lion cult, and there are statues of lions which stand guard over springs and fountains. In Greek myth, Cyrene was a water nymph who subdued lions, and whose great sanctuary was established around a spring.

The link with the dead is particularly evident in the common use of lion symbolism on grave markers, particularly in and around Athens. During the 4th century BC, some of the largest free-standing Athenian monuments ever produced took the shape of huge lions, carved from great slabs of marble, and weighing up to four or five tons. These funerary lions have been found at the famed Kerameikos cemetery, just outside the ancient city walls, and also commemorating tombs which originally flanked the ancient roads leading to Athens. These impressive feline monuments served as the symbolic protectors of tombs and as metaphors for the noble courage of the deceased. The most famous example of this tradition is the impressive marble lion which still marks the final resting place of the Theban Sacred Band, who fell in battle against Philip of Macedon and his son Alexander the Great at Chaeronea in 338 BC. This funerary use of the lion's image is another ancient survival, as can be seen in the many local and national commemorative monuments to those who died in the two world wars of the 20th century.

Fabulous cat-like beasts

The most dramatic and enduring legacy of the Greek use of feline symbolism was the startling artistic elaboration of the animal's shape to create fabulous mythological beasts. Such were the sphinx, griffin and chimaera, where parts of natural animals were torn from their original form and recombined as fantastic creatures to represent such qualities as intelligence, strength, dread and divinity.

Like its Egyptian prototype, the Greek sphinx had the body of a lion and the face of a human, and represented a predatory creature sent from the Underworld to terrorize and devour the inhabitants of Thebes until Oedipus correctly answered its riddle. Because of its association with violence and warfare, the sphinx was also an appropriate decorative motif for the helmet of Athena, the patron goddess and warrior-guardian of Athens. A connection with death, possibly as a protector against evil spirits, is implied by its widespread appearance on grave markers.

The griffin, similar to the sphinx in many ways, was generally shown with a winged lion's body and the face or beak of an eagle – features which, for the Greeks, naturally related the creature to soul birds and sirens, and to the terror inspired by death. The griffin made its home far to the north of Greece, in the country of the Hyperboreans, where it guarded a great golden treasure. Zeus and Hera were believed to have kept griffins as their 'sharp-beaked hounds', which may explain why many griffin decorations have been found at the sanctuaries of these deities at Olympia and on the island of Samos where they originally adorned huge bronze cauldrons.

According to Homer, the fire-breathing chimaera combined the elements of three animals. It is depicted in art either with three heads – of a lion, a goat and a serpent – or with a composite body, with lion fore-parts, goat middle, and serpent hind-parts. In myth, the chimaera lived on a mountain top in Lycia, southwest Turkey, and was killed by Bellerophon riding Pegasus, the winged horse which had been tamed by Athena. This connection may account for the many terracotta chimaeras which have been found at Athena's sanctuary at Gortyn on the island of Crete. So fantastical was the chimaera that the word *chimera* has come to mean anything wild or fanciful.

These images blended the natural with the imaginary and produced a unique, and specifically Greek, group of cat creatures. Regarded as agents of terror, these awe-inspiring beasts possessed supernatural abilities, took advantage of human weaknesses, and killed by violence and guile. Their iconographic use on grave markers, weapons, and as guardians of sanctuaries signify their intimate association with the realm of the dead.

Artistic traditions in which strange fabulous creatures played a central role have also survived in other parts of the world. Around 3,000 years ago, in ancient Peru, artisans of the early cult centre at Chavín de Huantar carved stone blocks and made pottery and sculptures which have preserved an extraordinary art style, depicting jaguars, caimans, serpents, eagles and humans in a dazzling array of forms. These composite feline creatures, deities perhaps of an ancient pantheon, are found in many places along the Pacific coast, painted on textiles or cast in gold. They retained their artistic popularity, and presumably their significance, through many subsequent civilizations. It has been suggested that the 'U' shape of many of Peru's ancient temples replicates the open maw of a jaguar, in the same way as the later Inca capital of Cuzco was said to be laid out in the form of a puma.

To the north of Peru, in the high mountain valleys of Colombia, sites such as San Agustín display an array of imposing stone sculptures which represent human bodies with fierce, snarling feline heads, or small feline alter egos perched protectively on the back of supposed chiefs or shamans. Further north still, in the swampy lowlands of eastern Mexico, where central America's first civilization flourished a millennium before Christ, a strong fascination with the jaguar was evident. Known as the Olmec, this early culture, like that of Chavín, produced enduring images of what were probably age-old beliefs. Olmec art – in stone sculpture, jade carving and cave painting – reveals what has been called the image of the were-jaguar: humans with strongly cat-like facial features. That such images belonged to an ancient civilization has led to the view that jaguar symbolism had an ideological message, linking the ruling elite with a mythical race of jaguar ancestors, which somehow legitimized their pre-eminent social position.

More recently, this link between the depiction of felines and their supernatural significance is particularly well illustrated among the North American Indians of the Great Lakes region. Here, designs showing supernatural feline figures were commonly found on buckskin and fibre pouches. Often highly stylized, and occasionally with buffalo horns added to create a fantastical horned-cat, these creatures are probably based on the Mountain Lion or puma – the largest feline predator of the region.

Puma imagery, thought to be related to myths of the supernatural Underwater Panther, Nampe'shiu, was used as decoration on the pouches in which shamans kept the ritual paraphernalia which allowed them to control the spirits of the hunt. Feline decoration thus linked the form and appearance of the bag with the function of the sacred and powerful materials which it contained, as well as with the status and power of the shaman himself. Similar imagery, also probably associated with shamanistic hunting rites, comes from the American Southwest, where the puma was regarded as a supreme hunter, associated with rain, fertility and warriors, and worshipped at special puma shrines, where the remains of its paws and hide, as well as stone fetishes carved as pumas, indicate ritual activity.

Northwards, on the Siberian side of the Bering Straits, the Nanai people of the Amur river basin wore amulets with tiger designs to ward off evil spirits, as part of a tiger cult whose ancient origins are implied by prehistoric petroglyphs. In eastern Siberia and Manchuria the shamans of the native Tungus peoples would placate a man-eating tiger by making a human sacrifice in which an unfortunate person was tied to a tree; if the tiger accepted the sacrifice, the tree was henceforth regarded as sacred.

Beliefs concerning the protective power of the tiger are also prevalent further south, where the Chinese have long regarded this great cat as the animal whose strength and ferocity frightens off evil spirits. As such, it is seen as the supreme guardian of graves. Ho Lü, the king of Wu between 513 and 494 BC, was buried in a tomb surmounted by a stone carving of a tiger. The famed tiger-jades were buried in graves on the right side of the corpse, facing west – the direction with which the tiger was cosmologically associated. According to the Chinese dictionary *Shuo wên*, of AD 100, tiger-jades are either jades upon which a tiger is carved or a jade carving in the shape of a tiger – in each case both substance and form were suffused with supernatural power. One legend recounts that tigers were tamed for the art of war, and that a tiger-jade could be used to mobilize an army.

Snarling tiger jaws are also thought to be an integral part of the famous *t'ao-t'ieh* or ogre masks, which had a magico-religious purpose and are found on bronzes and other tomb goods. Bronze artefacts from the Shang dynasty depict humans with ferocious tiger-like creatures, usually with their heads almost or actually in the cats' jaws. These art forms are thought to have been ritual paraphernalia, used in ceremonies which brought the dead and the living into a heaven and earth communication. Whatever their exact significance, it is a fact that the beasts depicted with humans on these bronzes are always tigers.

Tamed but Free

Cats of all sizes are models of self-reliance, and perhaps part of the attraction of the domestic variety is that it retains a strong streak of independence, despite its close relationship with people. Believed to have been the last common animal to be tamed, it is arguable to what extent the cat can really be called domesticated. Pet cats can undoubtedly be affectionate, but they remain untrainable, and are perfectly capable of living with or without human attention, as the increasing number of stray and feral cats demonstrates. It may be more accurate, as Roger Tabor notes in his book *The Wild Life of the Domestic Cat*, to say that they are tractable rather than fully domesticated – free ranging and home-loving at the same time.

Keeping cats as pets involves varying degrees of taming, and throughout history different societies have displayed a variety of attitudes to this practice. A tame cat is not necessarily a domesticated cat, but could, for example, be a cheetah or leopard used by humans in hunting, or a lion displayed in a circus. There are various ways in which cats may be tamed: they may be naturally or deliberately attracted to the warmth and food offered by human settlements, and so become accustomed to human presence. In time they may be become partly, but never totally, dependent on humans providing food, and, in the case of the smaller, less dangerous, varieties, become true pets. In other cases, particularly with the big cats, adults or cubs may be captured from the wild, raised and tamed for a specific purpose. The boundary between the tamed feline and the pet cat is indistinct – all cats can be tamed to a degree, but not all tamed cats are pets. By the same token, not all domesticated cats are pets either, as they may revert to a semi-wild, feral, state.

The territory of the tame cat, therefore, is defined by the prevailing cultural attitudes towards animals in general and felines in particular; it encompasses several overlapping physical and psychological landscapes, with each affecting the other by virtue of the ability of the human imagination to see connections and make analogies between the activities of people and those of cats. A black cat, for instance, may be regarded as a good 'ratter', an affectionate pet, a transformed witch or a symbol of bad, or perhaps good, luck. Similarly, a tiger may be regarded as a habitual man-eater, a royal game animal, a danger to livestock or a suitable heraldic emblem. Among some Amazonian Indians, domestic cats, ocelot and margay are kept side by side as valued and affectionate pets. Every human society makes its own choices in selecting which animals may share the domestic territory of the village, hut or penthouse suite, and individual and cultural factors all play a part in such decisions.

The fact that human attitudes towards cats reflect the prevailing social climate was nowhere more evident than during the Middle Ages in Europe, where the small domesticated cat had, hitherto, been kept less for human company than to keep down rats and mice. Some owners deliberately starved their cats to make them more enthusiastic hunters. Not long before, cats had been the only animals allowed into monasteries and nunneries, partly to catch rodents, but also to provide fur for clothing. With the advent of the 16th-century Witch Craze, however, the status of cats underwent a dramatic change, and they became associated with sorcery and magic, and were often identified as the spirit-familiars of witches.

The choice of the cat as the witch's helper was understandable. It matched the animal's natural behaviour (and its ambivalent status – domestic but not fully domesticated) with the anti-social activities of the mainly old women who were accused of witchcraft – at least in the minds of their accusers. Unlike dogs, cats cannot be trained; they fend for themselves, and constantly cross the boundary between their home base and the outside world. This point is well illustrated by the case of an old woman from the English county of Exeter, who was condemned to hanging on the testimony of a neighbour, who said that she had witnessed a cat jumping through the window of the woman's cottage and believed that it was the Devil. In the hysteria of the time, even the appearance of the cat was thought to indicate the presence of evil, as the animal's shining eyes were said to glow with the fires of hell. This phenomenon so impressed the French that they coined a word to describe it: *chatoyer*, 'to shine like a cat's eyes'.

The close relationship between cats and witches was widespread throughout the British Isles and Europe between the middle of the 16th and the end of the 17th centuries. In Scotland, cats were commonly regarded as witches in disguise or perhaps as the Devil himself. Scottish witches were accused of riding cats on their way to the sabbat and of being able to take on the shape of a cat. Many witches were believed to have an extra nipple which they used exclusively to suckle their diabolical companion. The still common saying, that a cat has nine lives, first appeared in 1584, in a book called *Beware of the Cat*, where nine was the number of times that a witch could take on feline shape.

Perhaps the most celebrated British case of cats associated with witchcraft occurred in 1566, with the trial of Elizabeth Francis, Agnes Waterhouse and Waterhouse's daughter Joan, at Chelmsford, Essex. Elizabeth apparently confessed to having been taught the black arts by her grandmother who had also given her a spotted cat named Sathan, a thinly disguised rendering of Satan. This devil in cat form was said to have been fed on bread, milk and Elizabeth's own blood, and she soon admitted to being able to speak with it. Sathan was believed to have been responsible for the death of one Andrew Byles, who, after having slept with the cat's mistress and made her pregnant, refused to marry her. This feline prince of devils told her how to abort her unwanted child and later also caused the death of another, legitimate, child. Elizabeth subsequently gave the devil-cat to Agnes Waterhouse, who promptly changed it into a toad, whereupon it caused the death of numerous cows and geese in the neighbourhood. Both Elizabeth and Agnes were later hanged for their activities – victims of a hysteria produced by shifting social conditions and religious beliefs.

By the beginning of the 18th century, the belief in witchcraft had waned, and attitudes towards cats changed significantly. As the historian Keith Thomas has said, the increasing popularity of cats probably also reflected the rising standard of domestic cleanliness, with cats, who constantly groom and clean themselves, being perceived as metaphors for cleanliness. Certainly, by the middle of the 19th century the cat population had risen dramatically, to perhaps one cat for every ten people – twice the number of dogs at the time.

Today, the domain of the most successful member of the cat family is the increasingly tamed environment of the owners' home and its immediate vicinity. As domestic cats possess no obvious economic value to their owners (indeed, it could be argued that they are a financial liability), it appears that they are kept for sheer enjoyment and companionship. In an increasingly industrialized and urbanized world, where families are often geographically separated, and people live longer, social life turns in upon itself, and domestic cats may satisfy an ever stronger social and psychological need for companionship. Whereas in previous times domestic cats may have been regarded as deities, wild spirits or pest controllers, today they may be substitutes for distant or deceased loved ones. Although the value of cats to humans as company cannot be denied, it is moot whether the cat feels the same way. A well-fed cat will wander less often and less far, and consequently spend more time with its owner – but is this true affection on the cat's behalf or mere self-interest?

The modern cult of the pet cat, and its close relation, the intense cross-breeding of different varieties, is a recent phenomenon. It began in 1871, when Harrison Weir, an artist and cat lover, held the first ever cat show at Crystal Palace in London. His aim was not, as later became the fashion, to run events for owners to win prizes, but to improve the lot of the common cat, and to ensure a wider appreciation of its nature, colour and markings. From these worthy beginnings the National Cat Club emerged in 1887, to be replaced by the Governing Council of the Cat Fancy in 1910.

At the time of the first cat show there were few breeds to chose from, but during the course of this century intensive breeding has developed numerous types of cat, resulting in different colour eyes and coats, length and type of fur, flattened faces and even an absence of tails. However, these differences are virtually all superficial. According to Juliet Clutton-Brock, a specialist in domesticated animals at the British Museum, underneath the often vivid surface, the 'designer cat' retains the skeletal structure which has always made it a superb hunting machine. This chameleon-like change of outward appearance is, in one sense, merely the latest manifestation of the magical shape-shifting that has always been associated with cats, both large and small. Whereas in ancient times such transformations occurred in the human imagination, and could only be made physical in art, today, the animal itself can be altered to suit different human temperaments and aspirations. Beneath it all, however, the cat remains the same, its essential nature unchanged. The modern cult of the pet cat, as part of a wider pet-keeping phenomenon, is unique in human history, and, in Europe alone, there are more than 23 million pet cats.

'The Sign of the Cat'

Cats of all sizes have never lost their attraction for human societies, and have proved to be ever popular icons, and rich and flexible metaphors, used to signify a range of human qualities, ideas and ideals, in a seemingly infinite variety of forms.

The ability of felines to adapt to a host of natural and artificial environments is matched by the equally diverse use which humans have made of the cat's image. In today's world, cats, like many other animals, have become a commodity, whose value to multi-national companies, advertising agencies, fashion houses and pet-food manufacturers, to mention just a few, may be seen as exploitation or good marketing, according to one's point of view. What is unquestioned is that the 'sign of the cat' is both potent and profitable, as, in a sense, it always has been.

The packaging of the domestic cat has led the way in the commercial exploitation of felines in recent years. Innumerable books relate the history of the cat, advise as to how it should be kept, treated, bred and presented in competitions. Cat calendars, accessories and clothing are just a few examples of the potential of the cat-lover's market, and an indication of the multi-million dollar nature of this modern cat cult.

The big cats, too, are amenable to glossy, status-related advertising and promotion. On the one hand there is the Jaguar, one of the world's most expensive and luxurious cars, owned and driven by those who wish to display their wealth and status in public. As a sign of the times, Jaguar donated a large sum of money to help preserve its original namesake, in the rainforests of Belize. If the image of the natural jaguar lends its kudos to car manufacture, then the petrol which powers it is not far behind. One of the most successful corporate logos of all time remains the Esso Tiger, conveyed into the living room by television, with a magnificent tiger bounding across the landscape in impressive slow motion, turning to confront the viewer as the advertisement ends. Ideas of strength, power and natural leadership are central to the images which such companies wish to convey, and, as we have seen, the large felines have been used in this way for countless millennia.

There exists today, as there probably always has, a contradiction at the heart of the relationship between human beings and cats. Although our society regards domestic cats as incomparable human companions, against which any cruelty is abhorred, attitudes to the big cats have been very different. Before the development of firearms, when man-feline confrontation involved a degree of personal bravery, skill and fear, there was a respectful relationship between the hunter and the hunted. Wearing the skin of a lion, tiger or leopard was a sign of achievement and status. With the arrival of the gun, however, killing at a distance removed this personal element, and so, much of its value. What had happened was that the symbolism of the feline had become a commodity, to such an extent that the prototype was in danger of becoming exterminated – the cultural image threatened to outlast the natural source of inspiration.

Big cats, particularly those with colourful coats, increasingly came to be seen as merely the intractable owners of beautiful pelts, which, it was thought, looked much better, firstly as hunting trophies, and secondly, and increasingly, when worn as a suitably tailored garment by women. The peculiarly Western notion that saw the wearing of such skins as an expression of glamorous female sexuality, led to the 'fur coat' becoming the ultimate goal of several generations of fashion-conscious women. The demand for such powerful and prestigious symbols of western womanhood, once stimulated, led to the indiscriminate slaughter of hundreds of thousands of their rightful owners, the virtual annihilation of some species, and to such incongruous images as that of a shapely fashion model draped in a leopard-skin coat caressing a pet cat.

However, as has been shown time and again, the treatment of cats reflects the prevailing social attitudes, and, in recent years, views have once again undergone dramatic change. In a world concerned with ecology, global warming and animal rights, the plight of the big cats, along with other endangered species, has become a focal point for changing human attitudes to a world which belongs to, and is shared by, all.

Today, royalty, politicians, the rich and the powerful cannot afford to be seen hunting the tiger or lion. The very individuals who, throughout history, were depicted in art and extolled in literature as the conquerors of dangerous feline foes, now distance themselves from such activities. Their relationship with the big cats has undergone a complete, if ironic, reversal, as the royal patronage of wildlife conservation movements and the financial support of government agencies and multi-national companies for conservation research illustrates. It is an interesting point to consider, that though the relationship between humans and the large felines has changed significantly, the metaphorical association between these majestic predators and the most influential and powerful segments of our society remains unchanged.

Hand in hand with the increasing awareness of conservationist issues have gone various national and international campaigns against the excesses of the fur trade. These have had considerable success, as the increasing amount of legislation and the overall drop in fur sales illustrates. Where once the display of such fashionable clothing attracted almost universal admiration and envy, in recent years it has come to symbolize the unthinking and commercial exploitation of the natural world and its inhabitants. The big cats and their skins have stayed the same, but the social values attached to them have changed out of all recognition. However, although the export and import trade in multicoloured cat skins is illegal, people still feel a strong attraction to clothing that at least *looks like* the real thing. Real skins may be 'out', but the welfare and survival of their natural owners are 'in'. The distinctive markings of the tiger, jaguar and leopard, applied to a variety of synthetic garments and accessories continue to be popular, an indication that the mystique of the cat remains today as powerful as ever.

Ancient images of magical beings haunt the art and sculpture of many of the world's great civilizations. Dangerous and predatory carnivores, such as the lion, were especially favoured to represent powerful anthropomorphic deities who either brought death and destruction or guarded against it. Nowhere is this better seen than in the imposing statues of Sekhmet, the lion-headed goddess of Dynastic Egypt. Worshipped as the daughter of the Sun god Ra in his temple at Heliopolis, Sekhmet was regarded as the 'Fiery One' who protected the universe by destroying her father's enemies. Her role as guardian-spirit was dramatically highlighted during the reign of Amenophis III, when the pharaoh commissioned some seven hundred statues of the goddess in a vain attempt to ward off a plague that was sweeping through the kingdom. (Statue of a seated lion goddess, Nekhen, Egypt)

The mirrored eyes of the jaguar are caused by a reflective layer of cells at the back of the eye which give America's largest cat superb 'night vision', and help it to hunt in the dark. This image of the mirror-eyed nocturnal predator inspired Central and South American Indians to spin a web of supernatural beliefs around the significance of mirrors, shiny surfaces (such as water), rock crystals, shadows and reflections. Shamans claimed to be able to see the future with 'jaguar eyes'. The realm of spirits was conceived as a parallel world, a mirror-image universe where the potent forces of nature were at the beck and call of the all-powerful, all-seeing jaguar.

The jaguar's likeness is still used in modern folk festivals. In rural communities in Mexico, springtime ceremonies are held to petition for rain and crop protection, and the jaguar or *tigre* mask is the most popular of all at such occasions. Many, like the one below, imitate the jaguar by having polished shell, mica or glass inserts in the eyes. (Wooden jaguar mask, Guerrero, Mexico; jaguar's eyes, caught in the flash from a camera)

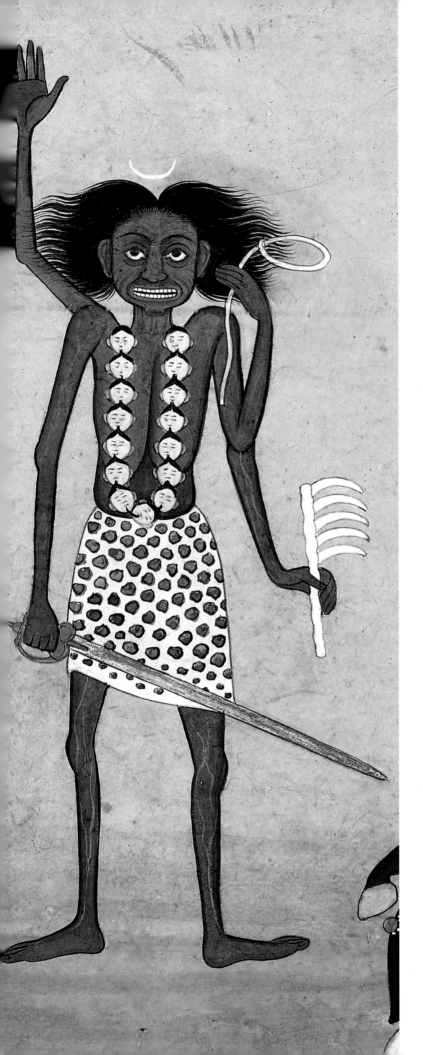

Feline imagery is a recurring theme in scenes concerned with warfare, retribution and sacrifice. Here, the Hindu Great Goddess, Durga, who represents the feminine force invoked by the gods, is seen with six arms, each signifying a different power. She rides into battle on a tiger, which itself takes part in the conflict by roaring at Durga's enemies. In front of the deity and her feline mount is the dark-coloured, leopard-skin-clad goddess Kali, a fierce aspect of Durga who emerges from the deity's frowning forehead wielding a sword. In Aztec Mexico, too, big cat symbolism was concerned with death and sacrifice, as the jaguar below, pierced by an arrow, illustrates. (Detail from an 18th-century painting, Kangra school; Codex Cospi, Mexico, Aztec period)

Lions were among the most popular decorative motifs for many of antiquity's craftsmen. Often paired with rulers and gods, they symbolized status, power and influence. The portrayal of the domination of Nature's fiercest predator by a king or ruler was an ancient metaphor for political and military control of subject peoples. That is why on this silver dish (above) the Sassanian ruler is shown standing on one lion and clasping two others by the mane.

The 7th-century BC hydra (opposite) shows an elaborate group of lions surrounding the winged goddess Orthia – the Spartan name for Artemis, the 'lone huntress'. (Silver dish, Sassanian period; bronze hydra, Sparta, c. 600 BC)

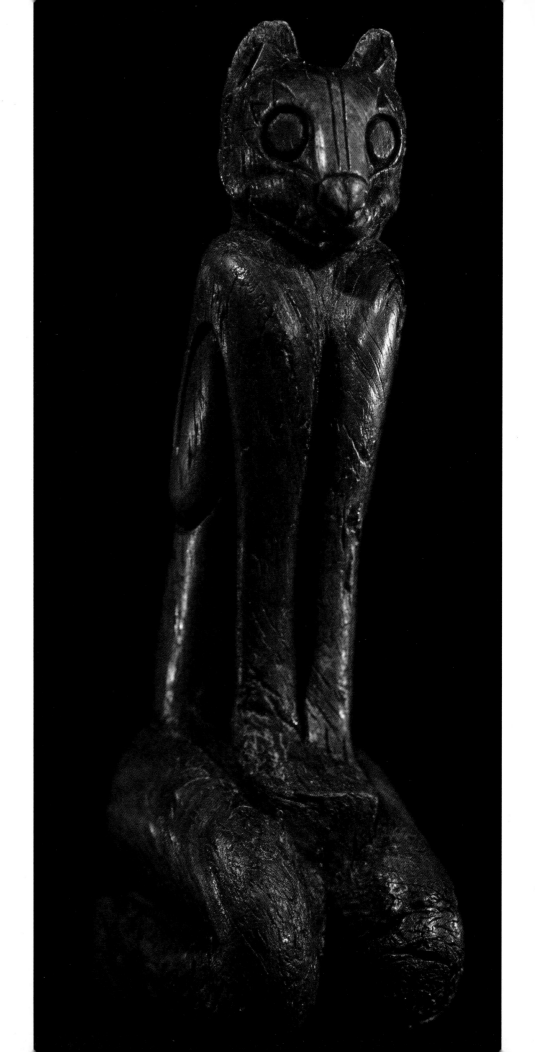

The imagination and artistic skills of Amerindian craftsmen rendered the cat's form in a variety of naturalistic, abstract and anthropomorphic images throughout the Americas. From an ancient Indian village at Key Marco, in southwest Florida, came this well preserved and powerful image of a kneeling feline figure (opposite). Possibly inspired by the puma, its distinctly human stance suggests that it may represent either a cat-shaman or perhaps an anthropomorphic feline spirit.

A different treatment (right) was accorded to the feline by the artists of the Late Paracas/ Proto Nazca people of the coast of southern Peru. Here, striking multi-coloured textiles depict fabulous feline creatures on a richly embroidered border which may originally have been part of a mummy bundle. (Carved wooden feline figurine, from Key Marco, Florida; embroidered textile, south coastal Peru, c. 300–1000)

Overleaf Domestic cats, and their habits, were undoubtedly well known in the Classical world. Pliny remarked on their stealth in stalking birds and mice, and they were probably kept more for vermin control than purely as pets. Artistic depictions are few, with the most familiar being this mosaic from Pompeii, which portrays a wide-eyed tabby cat pouncing on a partridge. (Cat and bird, Roman mosaic)

While big cats have always enjoyed a special relationship with humans, that between man and cheetah is unique. Often misleadingly known as the 'hunting leopard', because of its spotted coat, the cheetah is the only large feline which does not attack humans. The fastest animal on earth, it can attain speeds of up to 65 miles per hour, outpacing even gazelles and racehorses. Its speed, combined with the fact that it is the most easily tamed of all the big cats, has made the cheetah a favourite hunting companion for humans.

A Mesopotamian seal, dating to the 3rd millennium BC, depicts a cheetah held on a leash with a hood over its head. Tamed hunting cheetahs were popular in Egypt, whence they were taken to Minoan Crete. In ancient Persia and Moghul India the rich and powerful often kept a string of these speedy cats for royal coursing events, with the valued predator being conveyed, blindfolded, by special carriage, and let loose only when prey was sighted. During the Renaissance, most Italian courts had their 'hunting leopards' on display, and in 1479 the Duke of Ferrara presented a beautiful specimen to King Louis XI of France, as an appropriately noble and symbolic gesture of deference. Three hundred years later, cheetahs were still considered suitable gifts for

royalty; when George III was presented with one in 1764, it was released in Windsor Great Park near a stag, to demonstrate its hunting prowess. George Stubbs commemorated the event by painting the scene below. An earlier and simpler portrayal of two coursing cheetahs (right) dates to around 1400 AD. (George Stubbs, *Cheetah and Stag with Two Indian Attendants*, c. 1764; *Two Cheetahs*, Lombard school, c. 1400)

The big cats often appear engaged in epic struggles with heroes, and as such were metaphors for the human domination of the natural world. In Classical Greece, Heracles was the archetypal hero, whose first superhuman task was to defeat the huge Nemean lion which was terrorizing ancient Argos. This he did by squeezing it to death, as shown on this Greek vase (below). Scenes portraying similar battles retained their popularity, as this 7th-century AD Byzantine silver dish

(below left) illustrates, with its depiction of 'David slaying the Lion'.

In South America, countless stories were told to the early European explorers about large man-eating jaguars which attacked the Indians as they cut wood or foraged in the jungle. Although such attacks doubtless occurred, the Indian's attitude towards the jaguar was less a fear of the real animal than a dread of sorcery by shamans who had changed into jaguar form. This late 17th-century illustration (left) depicts an Indian woodcutter on the coast of Surinam, north-east South America, being attacked by a large jaguar with a suspiciously human-like stance and build. (Jaguar attacking Indian, from *Amerikaansche Voyagien*, A. van Berkel, 1695; Byzantine silver dish showing David slaying the Lion; unprovenanced Greek vase showing Heracles slaying the Nemean Lion, 6th century)

Overleaf The violent nature of the tiger has been a colourful source of inspiration for many artists. In Rousseau's *Tropical Storm with a Tiger* (left), the animal's ferocity is expressed metaphorically by the raw untamed forces of Nature. More direct is this detail from the 18th-century painting *Raja Umed Singh of Kotah Shooting Tiger* (right). (Henri Rousseau, *Tropical Storm with a Tiger*, 1891; *Raja Umed Singh of Kotah Shooting Tiger*, Rajasthani school, c. 1780)

Henri Roousseau
1 8 9 1

The style, subject matter and monumentality of early Greek sculpture owed much to the prior artistic achievements of ancient Egyptian civilization, where impressive rows of stone lions and sphinxes formed great avenues leading to sacred places. Inspired by such tradition this elongated but majestic marble lion (right) is one of a number which flank the ceremonial approach to the sanctuary of Leto in the Cycladic island of Delos, and dates to 575–550 BC.

The cult of the cat goddess Bastet, however, was uniquely Egyptian. Regarded as her representatives, pet cats were lavishly treated in life and their death was followed by elaborate mourning. Their remains were mummified and interred in cat-shaped caskets in cemeteries sacred to Bastet. This particular example (far right), one of thousands discovered over the past two hundred years, is dated to the Roman period around 200 BC. (Marble lion sculpture, part of a ceremonial avenue on Delos; mummified cat from Abydos)

The tiger, Asia's largest cat, is an indomitable hunter. It strength and ferocity, combined with its dramatic appearance, led to the use of its skin or image by sorcerers, priests, rulers and artists from China to India. This late 18th-century Japanese silk painting (opposite) captures not only the physical qualities of the tiger, but its almost supernatural essence as well. The otherworldly presence equated the majesty of this big cat with that of royalty, in symbols which expressed physical strength and protective spirit-power, as in this example of a Tibetan tiger rug (above). Emphasizing its role as spiritual guardian of the Tibetan elite, the craftsman has highlighted the tiger's fangs and claws, and given the animal a distinctly human face. (Kishu Ganku, *Tiger by a Torrent, c.* 1795; Tibetan tiger rug)

54

Scenes portraying big cats as man-eaters are not always what they seem. This ceramic effigy jar (opposite) from the Mochica culture of northern coastal Peru (c. 600 AD) shows a large standing feline rearing menacingly over the shoulder of a seated man. A military society, the Mochica may have sacrificed their prisoners of war to captive jaguars or pumas especially reared for the purpose, and this individual sports the distinctive hairstyle peculiar to such sacrificial victims. Whether this scene depicts such an event or perhaps signifies that the big cat is the man's spirit-protector is debatable.

In India, though tigers sometimes became feared man-eaters, this colourful carving of a tiger attacking a British soldier (below) is unique. Known as Tipu's Tiger, it is in fact a mechanical model, inside which is an organ that imitates the sounds of a tiger's roar and the cries of the unfortunate victim. Captured from a rebellious Indian ruler, it was displayed by the East India Company in London in 1800 – an amusing but potent reminder that Britain could subdue both real tigers and tigers as metaphors for exotic peoples and their rulers. (Jaguar attacking man, Mochica culture, Peru; Tipu's Tiger, model of tiger mauling English soldier)

The artist's rendering of the feline image has been as imaginative as it has been diverse, from medieval European cats in bestiaries (above), to the strange, fabulous, lion-like beasts (opposite), which were placed on the tops of Chinese coffins to stop the spirits of the dead emerging to harm the living. (Three Cats and a Rat, English ms. illustration, 13th century; Chinese ceramic demon, T'ang period)

Who is to say what is real and what a dream? Images and experiences gathered during waking hours combine and recombine in sleep to create scenes of a subconscious world of fear or pleasure. In *Portrait of a Little Girl* (below), Fred Aris created a strange landscape dominated by the surreal eyes of the little girl and the black cat she holds. Questions abound – is the cat her runaway pet, a stray she encountered in the forest, and what is such a smartly dressed child doing alone in such a place? More disturbing still is the oil painting *Wild Beast Wood* by Sidney Sime (opposite) – a hauntingly evocative image of an unnatural pack of fiery-eyed felines emerging from a primeval forest. Trees, darkness and moonshadow combine with the purposeful stealth of the big cats to produce an eerie, almost nightmarish scene. (Fred Aris, *Portrait of a Little Girl*, c. 1969; Sidney Sime, *Wild Beast Wood*, 1926)

Brightly coloured and distinctively marked, the mottled skins of leopards have been worn by humans probably since the Stone Age. In the tomb of Tutankhamun, his successor, King Ay, is seen draped in the leopard skin of the *setem* priests who officiated at funerary rituals (right). A world away in time and meaning is this leopard-print dress designed by Yves Saint Laurent in 1983 (opposite) – an image of 20th-century western female chic. (Drawing by Nadja Fejto of Yves Saint Laurent leopard-print dress; wall painting in the tomb of Tutankhamun, 14th century BC)

Since the dawn of civilization the lion has signified sexuality, death and spirit-power, in the artistic, mythic and magical traditions of many cultures. In medieval astrology, the sun represents the vital qualities of man, and so its zodiacal position at the time of birth is of prime importance. In this miniature (below), man is represented as the King of Creation, just as the lion beneath his feet is 'King of Beasts', and the astrological sign for the sun symbolizes the source of male virility.

In ancient Sumeria, the lion was associated with the female essence. This terracotta plaque of the 2nd millennium BC (opposite) shows the malevolent winged goddess Lilitu standing with taloned feet on either 'two lions or one lion with two heads. Later to become the Biblical Lilith, this most terrifying of Sumerian demons was also known as the 'Bringer of Death' and is regarded as a prototype for the medieval witch. (Sol, ms. illustration from *De Sphaera*, 15th century; Lilitu, Sumerian terracotta plaque)

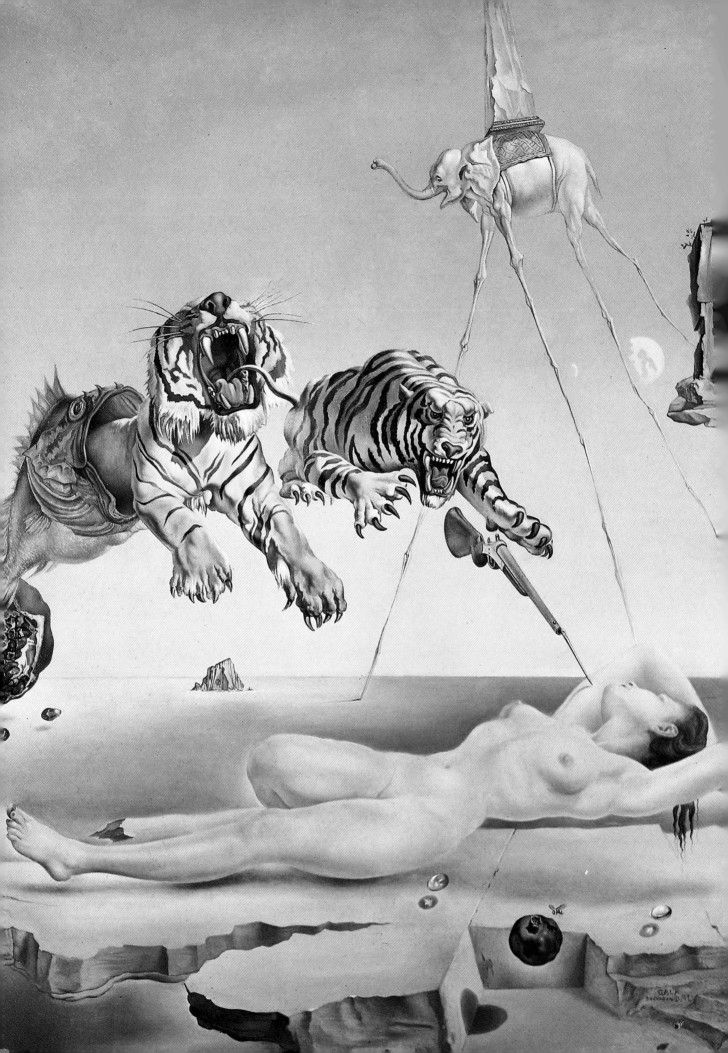

An emblem of supernatural power and authority from ancient South America, this carved wood head, with eyes and fangs of shell inlay, is believed to represent a fierce jaguar deity of the Mochica people, who flourished around the 6th and 7th centuries AD on Peru's north coast. Originally part of a ceremonial staff or handle, the image wears a jaguar headdress, illustrating not only the fascination of the feline for many Pre-Columbian civilizations but also the widespread use of big cats as status symbols. (Top part of ceremonial staff, Mochica culture, 6th and 7th centuries AD, National Museum of Anthropology and Archaeology, Lima, Peru)

In this picture by Salvador Dalí, *Dream Caused by the Flight of a Bee around a Pomegranate a Second before Awakening*, the artist reveals not only his genius, but his conscious and subconscious influences. Following Freud's psychoanalytic approach to dream symbolism, Dalí says of this piece that the fish stands for male potency, the rifle and bayonet for the phallus, the pomegranate is a symbol of female fertility and the two tigers embody unconscious urges that have been woken. The scene supposedly represents the sleeping woman's subconscious wish for intercourse.

Whatever Dalí or Freud might have said about this painting, its juxtaposition of large felines with a naked woman emphasizes the peculiarly Western 20th-century association of big cats with decorative skins and human female sexuality. It is also interesting to note that, at the time this painting was made, tiger and leopard skins were fashionable garments for women. (Salvador Dalí, *Dream Caused by the Flight of a Bee around a Pomegranate a Second before Awakening*, 1944)

Spirit of the Jaguar

For 10,000 years the jaguar has been the largest and most dangerous of America's big cats and since the beginning of Pre-Columbian civilization has been a recurring motif in the art and religion of Central and South American Indian societies. Jaguar symbolism permeated the religious thinking and creative activities of Mexico's first civilization, the Olmec. Flourishing in the tropical swamplands of eastern Mexico between 1250 and 400 BC, the Olmec were master carvers of jade and other greenstones and also made monumental stone carvings to adorn their temple-cities. Jaguars sometimes appear naturalistically in their stonework or cave paintings, but are more often portrayed as anthropomorphic figures, perhaps representing the mythological ancestors of Olmec royalty. These half-human, half-jaguar beings have been labelled 'were-jaguars', and an intriguing example of such a creature is this figurine (*left*), which has eyes inlaid with pyrites – to make them glow like a jaguar's eyes – paw prints incised on the bottoms of the feet, and traces of red cinnabar on the body. (Were-jaguar serpentine figure, Dumbarton Oaks Research Library and Collections, Washington, D.C.)

Many subsequent Mexican civilizations also used the jaguar icon to symbolize royalty, warfare and sacrifice. For the Aztecs, jaguar symbolism was closely associated with rulership and the élite warrior societies which protected and extended the empire. In this illustration (*below*) the ritual sacrifice of a prisoner of war is shown. Tied to a sacred stone, and armed only with a feathered stick, the victim is confronted by a warrior from the élite 'Jaguar Society', wearing a jaguar-skin suit of armour and wielding a sword. After having been slashed repeatedly, the prisoner was taken away to have this heart cut out and offered to the Aztec gods. (Aztec Codex Magliabecchiano, 16th century)

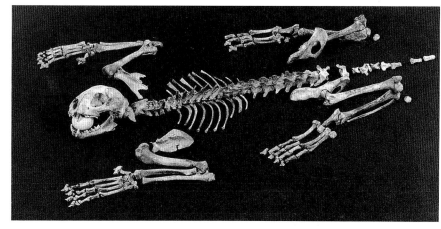

The jaguar's association with the symbolic equation between blood sacrifice, rainfall and fertility is seen to particular advantage in the jaguar skeleton (*above right*). Grasped firmly between the jaguar's jaws is a greenstone ball, which the Aztecs believed to symbolize 'solid rain'. (Jaguar skeleton from Chamber II of the Stage IV Temple, Aztec Great Temple, Mexico City)

In South America, many civilizations used the jaguar as an emblem of supernatural power and prestige. From

the Chavin culture, c. 850–200 BC, comes this Chavin priest or shaman (*above left*), wearing jaguar and serpent regalia, and grasping what is thought to be an hallucinogenic San Pedro cactus. Even today, the surviving peoples of the Tropical Rainforest use such hallucinogens and associate them with the jaguar, as is shown by the Guahibo shaman's narcotic snuff container (*below left*) made from jaguar bone. (Drawing of man as jaguar; drawing of Guahibo shaman's snuff container, Northwest

South America, after Reichel-Dolmatoff)

The jaguar's spirit was considered to be indomitable and its image was thought to protect against all other malevolent forces. In this photograph (*below centre*) of the now extinct Héta Indians of Paraguay, a shaman is seen curing a patient who is seated on one jaguar skin by waving a second skin over him. And (*below*) a shaman of the Brazilian Bororo tribe wears his 'jaguar impersonator's cape', made from several large pelts. (Curing the sick with jaguar skin; jaguar impersonator)

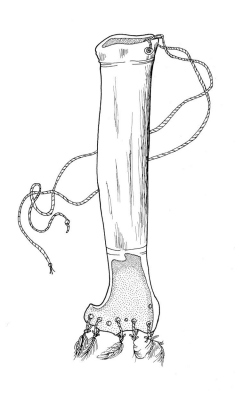

Cat Worship

In the ancient world, the image of the feline was a common motif in art and mythology, but real cat worship as such was a rarity. Only in Dynastic Egypt, with its distinctive tradition of animal worship, were felines transformed into gods and worshipped in their own right. The lion had always been a force to be reckoned with by the peoples who settled the fertile banks and delta of the Nile, and their lion goddess, Sekhmet (*left*), who combined a human body with a lion's head, was a vigorous deity who was invoked as the destroyer of the Sun god's enemies and as the guardian figure who protected against evil spirits, disaster and plague. (Black granite figure of Sekhmet, 22nd Dynasty, c. 930 BC, British Museum, London)

Sekhmet's magical powers were shared by her sister, the cat-headed goddess Bastet, but the latter was considered a more benign deity, associated with fertility and maternity. Egyptians believed that her image had the power to serve as a charm against misfortune. Typically, as in this Roman period figurine (*right*), she carried a basket, and wielded a shield as well as a magic rattle or sistrum with which she repelled evil spirits. (Statuette of Bastet, Egypt, c. 713-331 BC, Staatliche Museen, Berlin)

It may have been the care and attention lavished on tamed wild cats by temple priests that led to the appearance of the truly domestic cat by around 1500 BC. The popularity of these newly 'created' pets is shown by the quantity and variety of their figurines (*right*), made in gold, bronze, bone, wood and even mud. Many were decorated with jewelry and donated to temples as votive offerings. (Bronze cat from Egypt, Roman period, after 30 BC, British Museum, London)

With the arrival of Christianity cat worship naturally disappeared. The late 12th-century Winchester Bible preserves an interesting case of Christian zealotry and misunderstanding about the now paganized cat (*below left*). It was mistakenly believed that the heretical Cathars, who were also identified with the Jews, owed their name to the Latin for cat, and that their rites involved the miraculous appearance of a monstrous black feline. This may explain the cat-idol in the depiction of Mattathias beheading the idolatrous Jew. (Frontispiece to Maccabees, Winchester Bible, f. 350v., W. Cathedral)

Today, although we do not worship felines in a religious sense, the attention which many pet cats and probably most pedigree cats receive verges on the cultic. The photograph (*below right*) shows the winner of the 1989 Supreme Cat award. ('Grand Champion Travel Jack', 1989)

Power and the Pelt

The pelts of the leopard, jaguar and tiger have always been especially valued, symbolizing beauty as well as potency. In Egypt the mottled pelt of the leopard was worn not only by the male 'priests of the dead', but also by women of the royal family (*right*). (Stela of Princess Neferetyabet, c. 2580 BC)

In India, Shiva, the pre-eminent Hindu god, appears seated upon a tiger or wearing a tiger or leopard skin (*below*). Shiva acquired the skin after defeating the beast which had been sent against him by jealous sages. (Shiva, Indian painting, c. 1740)

The same association between the deities and the large cats is found in Greek religion. The god Dionysus is often depicted riding a leopard (*above*). (Mosaic of Dionysus, Delos, Greece, c. 100 BC)

A world away, in Aztec Mexico, it was the brightly coloured pelt of the jaguar which represented royal power in the costumes of the élite and as a covering for the emperor's throne. Aztec rulers were regarded as the embodiment of their supreme deity, Tezcatlipoca, a god who could manifest himself as a huge jaguar and was believed to dwell in the heart of the mountain. At his coronation, while seated on a jaguar-skin cushion or throne, a new emperor would pierce his skin with a pointed jaguar bone and draw blood as a ritual offering to the deities. In this illustrated manuscript (below) the Aztec emperor Acamapichtli is shown standing next to his large jaguar-throne. (Aztec ruler Acamapichtli, 16th century)

For traditional African societies, leopard symbolism is a recurring emblem of physical strength and spiritual power even today. Among the Nuer, a cattle herding people of the Southern Sudan (above), such symbolism is associated particularly with the fertility of the land. In Nuer society, the leopard-skin priest has clearly defined ritual duties and a deep symbolic attachment to the soil.

This ancient connection between the leopard and crop fertility survives to produce strange and contradictory images. In 1988, during a papal visit to Maputo in Mozambique, Pope John Paul II conducted a Holy Mass in robes trimmed with leopard-skin patterned cloth, and received gifts of fruit and a chalice from local women in return for dispensing gold coins (left). (Nuer leopard-skin chief; Pope John Paul II, Maputo, Africa, 1988)

The Royal Foe

Alexander the Great, depicted (*above*) in some danger during a lion hunt in the Macedonian capital of Pella, had conquered the known world from Greece to India by the time of his early death. As 'King of Asia', he took over some of the attributes of his Persian predecessor, Darius the Great, shown (*far left*) shooting at lions from his chariot. (Pebble mosaic, Pella, Greece, 300 BC; royal seal of Darius, Persian, 6th–5th century BC, British Museum, London)

Alexander also compared himself to Heracles, and was often depicted wearing the heroic lion-skin headdress (*below*). Heracles himself defeated the Nemean lion (*bottom left*) and thereafter wore its skin (*centre left*). (Medallion, Tarsos treasure, first half of 3rd century AD, Cabinet des Médailles, Paris; silver dish, 6th century AD, Bibliothèque Nationale, Paris; detail of a vase by the Berlin painter, c. 480 BC, Antiken Museum, Basel)

The lion, the 'King of Beasts', has been a symbol of royalty since the dawn of civilization. Heroes and kings are depicted defeating the 'royal foe' in either elaborate hunting scenes or epic single-handed battles. The privilege of hunting the lion was restricted to royalty; they alone were believed to possess the social prestige and physical prowess required to subdue it. After its death, the lion's qualities and appearance were assumed by its vanquisher, as a measure of his earthly and divine achievement.

Lion-hunting was thus considered a noble sport, which required qualities of bravery and leadership akin to those used in war. A king's domination over lions was an expression of his military prowess and divine right to rule. The stone relief (*above*) of a dying lion is from the great northwest palace of Assurbanipal in the Assyrian city of Nineveh. The rest of the panel shows the Assyrian king slaying numerous large maned lions and celebrating their defeat. (Assyrian stone relief, c. 645 BC)

As we have seen (*opposite page*), it is Heracles who represents the most famous example of man-lion confrontation. Heracles began his rise to mythic immortality by overcoming the deadly Nemean lion. This great beast, born of the hundred-headed Typhon, terrorized the Peloponnese region until Heracles squeezed it to death, skinned it with its own claws, and wore its pelt as a sign of his superhuman victory – the first of his 'twelve labours'. Lions undoubtedly posed real threats to livestock in early Greece, and the Heracles myth probably embodied many actual as well as imaginary events.

For the artists of antiquity, the lion symbolized strength and power, but this depiction of the death of Milo (*below*) drapes the Greek hero in the more colourful leopard skin. A 6th-century BC athlete, Milo of Croton was crowned six times at the Olympic games, and was known throughout the ancient world for his feats of strength. He met a premature death when a tree he was trying to render apart closed on his hand, trapping him until wolves tore him to pieces. (Jean-Jacques Bachelier, 1724–1806, *Death of Milo of Croton*, National Gallery of Ireland, Dublin)

Sphinxes and Winged Beasts

The sphinx combines a lion's body with a human head. The best known sphinx is the one next to the pyramids at Giza (*above*). Some 240 feet long, it was commissioned by the pharoah Chephren in the 3rd millennium BC. (Sphinx with the pyramids of Chephren, 4th Dynasty, Giza)

Almost two thousand years later, a sphinx from the Nile delta (*far left*) shows the pharoah Amenemhet III, his distinctive features neatly fitted into a beautifully rendered, maned lion. And as late as 1869 the symbolic association of the sphinx with Egypt reappears in a medal (*left*) struck to commemorate the opening of the Suez Canal. (Sphinx of King Amenemhet III, Tanis, 507 BC, Cairo Museum; Austrian medal 1869)

The connection between winged sphinxes, royalty and the gods is revealed (*right*) in the two winged sphinxes at Susa, the administrative capital of the Achaemenid dynasty, which are overlooked by the winged disc of the supreme creator god, Ahuramazda. The fall of the Persian empire to Alexander the Great was followed by the rise of the Parthian civilization and then the Sassanian culture, around 224 AD. The Sassanians also retained some of the mythological symbols of their predecessors, such as this female figure (*centre below*) riding a fabulous winged sphinx. (Persian sphinxes, Achaemenid period enamelled brick bas-relief, Louvre, Paris; female figure on winged beast, silver and gilt plate, Iranian, 7th century, Metropolitan Museum, New York)

A uniquely Greek variation of the sphinx was the fire-breathing feline monster known as the chimaera, a lion with a serpent's tail and a goat's head growing out of its back. It was slain by Bellerophon riding the winged horse,

Pegasus (*above*). Classical Greek influence extended to the Etruscans in Italy. This superb bronze chimaera (*right*) was discovered in Arezzo in the 16th century. (Bellerophon and Pegasus, Melian terracotta relief, c. 475–450 BC, British Museum, London; Etruscan bronze chimaera, Museo Archeologico, Florence)

In *fin-de-siècle* Europe, the sphinx took on erotic overtones not present in ancient art (*left*). (F. Khnopff, *The Caresses of the Sphinx*, 1896, Musée Royal des Beaux Arts, Brussels)

The Lion of War

The lion has always been the symbol of
the patriotic spirit of the dead, and of
ethnic or national pride in the
achievements of rulers and their
subjects. Its image has often marked
those monuments that commemorate
young men sacrificed in war. On these
final resting places the implacable lion
embodied the nation's gratitude for
martial efforts, but also protected the
dead from evil spirits which could
disturb their rest.

The symbolic funerary lion was a
well-known sight in the Classical world.
The most famous of all such
monumental felines is from the
battlefield of Chaeronea in central
Greece (*right*). It marks the final resting
place of the Theban Sacred Band who,
after refusing to surrender, fought to
the last man against the army of Philip
of Macedon in 338 BC. (Lion tomb,
Chaeronea, Greece)

The relationship between lions,
strength and patriotic fervour appears
often on medals and coins struck to
record famous victories, such as
Cromwell's at the battle of Dunbar in
1651 (*far left*) and Wellington's success
at Seringapatam in India in 1799 (*left*). In
the former, the Scottish lion holds the
thistle; in the latter, beneath a swirling
Union Jack, the 'British Lion' triumphs
over the 'Indian Tiger' – each animal a
metaphor for the country and rulers it
represents. (Medal commemorating
Cromwell's victory at Dunbar, 1651;
medal commemorating Wellington's
victor at Seringapatam, 1799, Apsley
House, London)

GOTT STRAFE ENGLAND !

1914-15

THE EMPIRE NEEDS MEN!

THE OVERSEAS STATES

All answer the call.
Helped by the **YOUNG LIONS**
The **OLD LION** defies his Foes.
ENLIST NOW.

The 'dying lion' (*below*) was carved from the living rock to commemorate the Swiss guards who fought and died for Louis XVI in Paris during the French revolution. (Monument to the Swiss guard, sculpture by Bertel Thorwaldsen, Lucerne, Switzerland)

The British acquisition of the African lion as its patriotic guardian emblem was accepted even by the country's enemies. During the First World War, anti-British posters in Germany (*above left*) showed the British lion struck low by a bolt of German lightning. The caption reads, 'May God Punish England'. (German First World War poster, Altonaer Museum, Hamburg)

In 1914, the British produced this recruitment poster (*left*) which neatly encapsulates several metaphorical elements; the maned British lion defies the enemy, but is helped by the massing figures of younger lions representing the patriotic manpower of empire. (British First World War poster, Imperial War Museum, London)

Guardians and Emblems

The guardian lion has been one of the most enduring feline emblems, as the spirit-force of the indomitable king of beasts was believed to reside in its varied images. One of the most spectacular examples is above the monumental entrance to the ancient city of Mycenae in Greece (*left*), where two guardian lions are carved out of a single block of stone. These royal protectors, made around 1250 BC, echo similar motifs from the Hittite cities of central Turkey, as well as this earlier terracotta lion from an ancient Mesopotamian city (*right*). Similar ideas had also existed from time immemorial in China, where lions and tigers were adopted as the spiritual protectors of both sacred and secular buildings (*top*). (Lion gate, Mycenae, *c.* 1250 BC; terracotta lion, Mesopotamia, *c.* 2000 BC, Iraq Museum, Baghdad; Chinese roof tile, 16th-17th century, The Burrell Collection, Glasgow)

The supernatural power ascribed to the guardian lion also crossed religious boundaries, as in this Ark of the Covenant (*below left*) flanked by two large lions in a scene that would have been understood a thousand years before Judaism. (Menorah on gold glass, Biblioteca Apostolica, Vatican, Rome)

In later times in Europe, strange images of historical personages were conjoined with a lion's body to create a sort of medieval sphinx, as with this mid-15th century image of Lord Hastings (*below*). (Emblem of Lord Hastings, *c.* 1466–70)

Wherever power, prestige and magnificence resided, the emblematic lion was also sure to dwell. In 1617, the king of beasts appeared as a magnificent 'Belgian Lion' map (*right*), which encompassed the seventeen provinces of the Netherlands. The lion of St Mark (*below*) was used to symbolize the wealth and success of the Venetian maritime empire. (Map of the Netherlands, from P. Montanus's *Germania Inferior*, 1617; Vittore Carpaccio, *The Lion of St Mark*, 1515, The Doge's Palace, Venice)

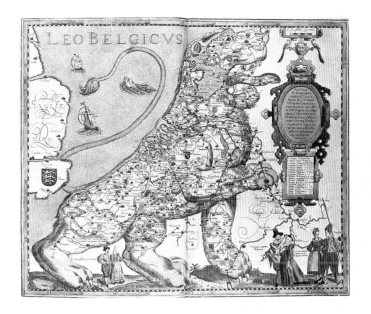

Even more successful than the Venetians, however, was the mainly 19th-century British empire. In keeping with at least three thousand years of imperial iconography, the British adopted the African lion as their distinctive emblem. It signified omnipotence and the 'god-given' right to rule vast tracts of the world. In 1865 Landseer was hard at work in his studio (*left*) producing one of the most enduring and loved emblems of empire – the four lions that would eventually become the guardians of Nelson's Column in Trafalgar Square.
(J. Ballantyne, *Sir Edwin Landseer in His Studio*, c. 1858, National Portrait Gallery, London)

Witchcraft

Witchcraft hysteria spread through Europe during the 16th and 17th centuries. The frequent identification of the European witch as an old woman, and of a black cat as her familiar, echoed similar liaisons in the Classical world between female deities and members of the cat family. In 16th-century Europe, however, the social, religious and cultural climate led to licentious or sinister interpretations being placed on quite innocent relationships between women and felines. Witches were often depicted naked (*left*), old, ugly or disabled (*opposite above*). The four witches (*left*) are seen preparing for a sabbat. One holds a cat, while in the foreground a cat-familiar consults a book of magic spells and diabolical incantations. (Hans Baldung Grien, 1484–1545, *Witches with Cat-Familiars*; English witches: Anne Baker, Joan Willimot, Ellen Greene, 1618)

The most famous witch's cat was Sathan (*below*), whose exploits figured prominently in the notorious Chelmsford witch trials of 1579. He was alleged to be the Devil in disguise, fed on his mistress's blood, and was able to converse with her in a 'hollow voice'. (Handcoloured print of demonic cat, 1579)

The European obsession with witchcraft and demonology was an integral part of the inquisitorial religious zeal which the Spanish took to the Americas. In this unique late 16th-century chronicle by the half-Spanish, half-Inca Poma de Ayala (*below left*), the plight of the conquered Peruvian Indian is highlighted by depicting the various Spanish officials as demons in the form of wild animals, such as the jaguar, puma, and the domestic cat. (*Nueva corónica*, by Guaman Poma, *Image of the New World*, London, p.77)

By the 18th century, however, the frontiers of superstition were being pushed back. A 1762 engraving by William Hogarth (*below right*) shows a witch riding her broomstick while suckling her cat with a 'third' nipple. This is not an illustration of a superstitious belief but a satirical attack on it. (W. Hogarth, *Credulity, Superstition and Fanaticism*, 1762, detail)

Training and Taming

Man has always sought to impose his order on the varied creatures which inhabit the natural world. Since lions, tigers and leopards, more than any other beasts, came to represent the raw untamed forces of nature, man could, by dominating these animals, set his indelible mark on the whole of creation.

The next step was to train or tame the big cats for human enlightenment or entertainment and no civilization produced more spectacular examples of big cat entertainment than the Romans. In the huge Colosseum in Rome daily events were staged to satisfy a bloodthirsty mob. Lion was pitted against leopard, leopard against gladiator. The big cats were brought into service as executioners – of Christians (*above*), criminals and defenceless prisoners (*below*). Gérôme's painting (*above*) shows Christian martyrs at prayer as the lions emerge to destroy them. (L. Gérôme, 1824–1904, *The Last Prayer*, Walters Art Gallery, Baltimore; Scene in the arena, Roman mosaic, c. 200 AD, Tripoli Museum)

Slowly, throughout the centuries, attitudes to nature and to animals changed, until today they are the exact opposite of what they were in the ancient world. The belief that humans had nothing to fear from even the largest and most dangerous animals led to such images as this painting by Landseer (*right*) of the lion tamer Isaac van Amburgh reclining in a cage containing peaceable lions, tigers, and leopards. (E. Landseer, 1802–73, *The Tamer Isaac van Amburgh with his Animals*, By Gracious Permission of Her Majesty the Queen)

The power of the big cats to kill any unprotected human being gave immense propaganda value to depictions showing man and animal together, with man as master, as in this painting (*above*), which expresses the title of the Ethiopian emperor as 'Lion of Judah', and in the Christian story of St Jerome and the Lion (*above right*) in which man's mastery of the wild feline symbolizes also the controlling of ungodly desires. (Emperor of Ethiopia with tame lions, Ethiopian folk painting; G. Bellini, *St Jerome in the Wilderness*, c. 1450, Barber Institute of Art, Birmingham)

Human control of the natural world could also have political overtones. This advertisement (*right*) emphasizes the friendship between the noble British lion and the Bengal tigress (Atkins's Royal Menagerie, early 19th-century advertisement)

A more recent image of fraternity between competing species comes from the film, *Born Free* (*below right*), based on the book by Joy Adamson, the naturalist and conservationist. Here, the young lion cub is being fed by Adamson, played by Virginia McKenna. (Virginia McKenna in *Born Free*, 1965)

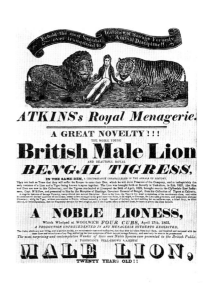

The Heraldic Lion

The heraldic lion, symbol of ferocity and strength, and hence of the power of warriors and kings, goes back to ancient Mesopotamia, Egypt and Greece. In the Echternach Gospels (*left*), painted in Northumbria in the 7th century, the lion of St Mark is already a stylized symbol expressive of the divine spirit. (Echternach Gospels, English 7th-century MS. Lat. 9389, f. 75v., Bibliothèque Nationale, Paris)

On the 12th-century coronation mantle of the Holy Roman Emperors (*below*), the lions assume their traditional posture of tearing their prey to pieces. During the Middle Ages, members of the nobility and the knightly orders adopted animals as heraldic devices to proclaim their rank and identity. The lion, king of beasts, was naturally associated with royalty. Used originally on the battlefield, their emblems became increasingly ceremonial and elaborate. (Coronation mantle of the Holy Roman Emperors, c. 1112, Kunsthistorisches Museum, Vienna)

The King of Scots (*right*) is an illustration for a book of armorial bearings made in France in the 15th century. The characteristic lion of Scotland appears on his caparison, shield, mantle and helmet. By this time the standard poses that could be adopted by a lion had been reduced to six: 'rampant' signified standing on its hind legs, claws extended. (King of Scots, illustration from Armorial de l'Europe et de la Toison d'Or, French, 15th century)

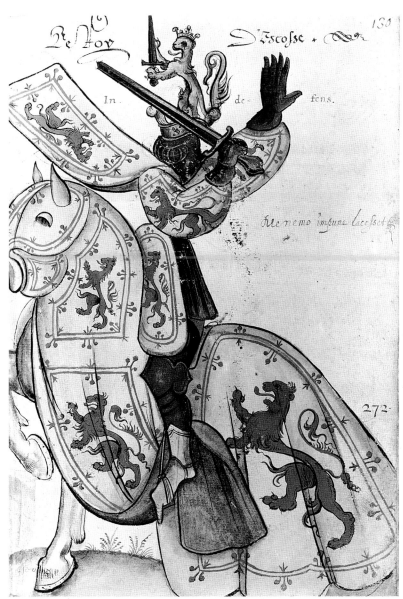

After the Age of Chivalry had passed, the rampant lion descended in the social scale and could be found functioning as an inn sign. Here, at the Hotel zum Löwen at Rothenburg-ob-der-Tauber, Germany (*above*), he holds the arms of the town of Rothenburg. At an even humbler level (*right*) is this docile creature, a sign painted for a New England tavern about 1815. (Hotel zum Löwen, Rothenburg-ob-der-Tauber, Germany; Goodwin Tavern sign by W. Rice, *c*. 1815, Wadsworth Atheneum, Hartford)

Astrology and Superstition

Across the millennia, astrological and occultic traditions have honoured felines with a celestial abode in the night sky. Leo is one of the twelve zodiacal constellations, an ancient identification that goes back at least to the Classical world and was recognized by the Arabs in this medieval astrological manuscript (*right*) which shows the 'Sign of the Lion', in which the king of beasts is seen carrying the sun on its back. (Medieval astrological ms by Abu Masher)

A combination of astronomical knowledge and astrological beliefs ascribed a 'feline influence' to the various calendars with which civilizations measured the passing of time, and calculated their agricultural year. It may be no accident that Leo presides over the summer months, since cats were associated with bringing rain and therefore increasing the fertility of the land. This early 15th-century French Book of Hours (*below right*) links the labours of the months – here harvesting – with the zodiac signs. (15th-century French ms illustration)

The fruitfulness of Mother Earth was extended to human mothers, and the fertile domestic cat became a metaphor, firstly for sexual activity and then for promiscuity – a belief probably traceable to Egypt, where the worship of the cat goddess Bastet incorporated the maternal hopes of Egyptian women. In later medieval times, the cat became a symbol of the sexual permissiveness of witches; later still, terms such as 'wildcat' and 'pussy' took on heavy sexual overtones. Brothels became known as 'cathouses' and promiscuity among men was referred to as 'tomcat' behaviour. Such connections are surely present in the etching by Gillray (*left*), in which a prostitute is seen at her toilet, watched by an animated cat. (James Gillray, *The Whore's Last Shift*, 1779)

Equally ancient in origin, and linked
in one sense to the cat's supernatural
and spiritual qualities, was the
relationship enjoyed by the feline and
soothsayers. In prehistoric times, such
an association was between the
sorcerer and his cat-familiar, but in
more recent times a variety of card
games have embraced a mixture of
superstition, arcane lore and cat-
inspired legends. In this evocative 19th-
century engraving, 'A Peep into
Futurity' (right), a young woman
interprets the fall of the cards, while
the inscrutable cat sits immovable,
contemplating the fire. (A Peep into
Futurity, after D. Maclise, 1806–70)

Most famous of all such card games
was the tarot, a recent version of which
shows a fantasy world protected by
panthers and inhabited by beautiful
people who hold cats in the highest
esteem. Card VII (right), known as 'The
Chariot', depicts a high-ranking stalwart
warrior carrying a cat banner and
wearing feline regalia on a chariot
drawn by a matched pair of cats. (Card
from Tarot of the Cat People, designed
by Karen Kuykendall, 1985)

Superstition is certainly still alive. The
good luck commonly ascribed today to
the black cat has been put to good use
by the owners of the Hyde Park Hotel
in London. Whenever thirteen guests
come to dinner, the proprietors bring
out a suitably attired black china cat
(far right), to move the number safely
up to fourteen. (China cat, Hyde Park
Hotel, London)

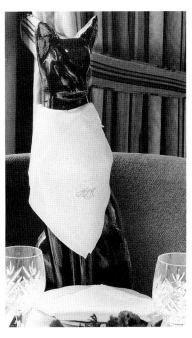

I'm Whittington's Cat as you plainly may see, — | Then keep me with care as a Friend ought to do
That famous Lord Mayor got his Fortune by me. | And I may perhaps get a Fortune for you.—
Painted for & Sold by CARRINGTON BOWLES, Nº 69 in St Pauls Church Yard, LONDON.

Cat Characters

Over the last two hundred years especially, when the domestic cat became more of a pet than a demon, a variety of cat figures became perennially popular literary characters. Appearing in what often survive as children's stories, they preserve grains of folk knowledge and perhaps ancient pagan beliefs about the significance of cats, and the good or bad luck they bring.

Two of the best known are Dick Whittington's cat (*above left*), and Puss in Boots (*left*), both of whom brought fame and fortune to their impoverished masters. The Cheshire Cat (*above*), a more ambiguous creature, was immortalized by John Tenniel in his illustrations to Lewis Carroll's *Alice's Adventures in Wonderland*. The phrase 'grin like a Cheshire cat', common in Carroll's day, is thought to derive from the grinning lions painted on inn signs by a Cheshire painter. (Dick Whittington's Cat, engraving published by Carrington Bowles, 1777; Puss in Boots, illustration by G. Doré, 1863, from Perrault's *Fairy Tales*; illustration by J. Tenniel from Lewis Carroll's *Alice's Adventures in Wonderland*, 1865)

A more accurate account of feline behaviour is Kipling's 'The Cat that Walked by Himself' (*right*), 'neither a friend nor a servant' to mankind. (Illustration by Rudyard Kipling to 'The Cat that Walked by Himself', *Just So Stories*, 1902)

C was a lovely Pussy Cat; its eyes were large & pale;
And on its back it had some stripes,
and several on his tail.

Edward Lear's cat from his *Comic Alphabet* of 1880 (*above*) is based on his own pet cat, 'Foss', which shared Lear's life in Italy and was eventually buried there. (Cat from Edward Lear's *Comic Alphabet*, 1880)

Despite the 19th century's tendency towards friendly, if ambiguous, cat images, 'The Black Cat' by Aubrey Beardsley is more sinister, in keeping with its purpose as an illustration for the works of Edgar Allan Poe (*right*). (Beardsley illustration, 1894, for Edgar Allan Poe's 'The Black Cat')

The Cat as Companion

The modern obsession with keeping pets, particularly cats, is all pervasive, and on a scale unique in human history. Stripped of any religious significance, the domestic cat remains an ambiguous creature. Sterilized, fed on demand and cossetted, it is, in a sense, not a natural creature at all, but a human creation. Yet it retains its independent soul and can always choose to return to the wild. Today, domestic cats are kept mainly for companionship – a solace to the old and childless, company for the lonely and an affectionate recipient of human kindness.

The origins of cat-keeping are as ambiguous as the animal itself. During the 15th and 16th centuries, when women of the lower classes who kept cats were considered to be witches and devil worshippers, there also existed cat-lovers among the well-to-do. Some, like the 3rd Earl of Southampton (*above*), were devoted to their pets. This portrait, painted around 1590, commemorates the Earl's stay in the Tower of London for his part in the Earl of Essex's rebellion. Eventually pardoned, this aristocratic patron of Shakespeare is portrayed with a sleek black and white cat which helped him endure his imprisonment. (*Portrait of 3rd Earl of Southampton*, attrib. John de Critz, *c.* 1554–1642, Collection of the Earl of Buccleuch)

By the beginning of the 18th century pet-keeping had become an English obsession. In fact cats were often treated and fed better than servants, and after death were ceremoniously buried and deeply grieved. The practice of dressing cats up in elaborate laces was also prevalent at this time. A painting by Joseph Wright of Derby (*left*) shows a kitten suffering this humiliation at the hands of its youthful owners. (Joseph Wright, *Dressing the Kitten*, 1771, Private Collection)

During the 19th century, the European domestic cat became firmly entrenched as part of everyday life, and was endlessly portrayed in a variety of scenes. From this time on there was a close and entirely innocent relationship between pet cats and women, with the cat viewed as a harmless and affectionate companion. Such intimacies are touchingly captured by Renoir (*right*). (Auguste Renoir, *Sleeping Girl with Kitten*, 1880, Sterling and Francine Clark Art Institute, Williamstown, Mass.)

Gwen John was later to paint a more poignant aspect of the companionable cat – that of solace for a lonely person (*above*). (Gwen John, *Young Woman Holding a Black Cat*, c. 1915, Tate Gallery, London)

Images of pet cats reflect not just the personality of their owners, but also the cultural attitudes of the time in which they were created. David Hockney's painting (*right*) presents a post-1960s image of an erstwhile hippy couple who now possess a well-groomed cat to complement both their lifestyle and the colour scheme of their home. (David Hockney, *Mr and Mrs Clark and Percy*, 1970–71, Tate Gallery, London)

Skinned

Natural camouflage served the great cats well, until the coming of man, when the feline's decorative pelt began to be worn by men and women as a sign of their physical and psychological domination of nature – a domination that was sealed irreversibly with the invention of firearms. The big cats had been hunted throughout antiquity, but it was the combination of technology and 19th-century British imperialism which brought felines such as the tiger and leopard to the brink of extinction.

Once a source of imperial pride and manly prowess, images of the successful hunter's 'achievements' have now become a record of ghastly European excess. In this picture from around 1900 (*above*), two white hunters are seen in front of a modest 'bag' of Indian tiger skins. (Tigershoot, from *A Sportswoman in India*, by Isabel Savory, 1900)

Metaphorical associations between the British and the big cats of empire also manifested themselves to lasting effect in military tradition and dress. The power, prestige and extent of empire is represented here by three British army drummers in a photograph taken during the 1920s (*left*). (Drummers, 1st Battalion, York and Lancaster Regiment, 1920s)

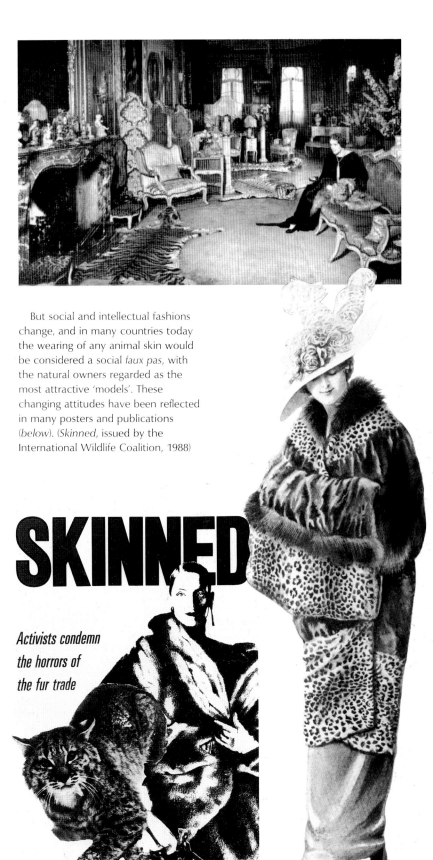

Similar imagery penetrated deep into the domestic British psyche, where the symbols of world conquest were transformed into fashionable clothing and adornments for the houses of the wealthy. In an 1895 photograph (*above*), Rudyard Kipling's daughter is seen cradled in an armchair draped with a tiger skin, and in a more exaggerated vein some forty years later, the romantic novelist Elinor Glyn was photographed surrounded by three tiger skins on the floor of her drawing room (*above right*). Although tiger pelts were considered eminently suitable as floor coverings, leopard skins were increasingly favoured as the basis for fashionable clothing (*far right*). (Kipling's daughter, Josephine, *c.* 1895; Elinor Glyn, 1936; Harrods catalogue, 1910)

But social and intellectual fashions change, and in many countries today the wearing of any animal skin would be considered a social *faux pas*, with the natural owners regarded as the most attractive 'models'. These changing attitudes have been reflected in many posters and publications (*below*). (*Skinned*, issued by the International Wildlife Coalition, 1988)

SKINNED

Activists condemn
the horrors of
the fur trade

The Sign of the Cat

The cat has always been a flexible vehicle for metaphor, and through the years its image has acquired new meanings and directions. It has most often stood for strength and prestige – and these characteristics have remained central to the modern use of the feline image.

The leaping jaguar (*above*) adopted as a logo by Jaguar Cars in the 1950s is just one of many examples of the use of the feline image to express strength, speed and quality. Similarly powerful is the Esso Tiger, one of the 20th century's most successful corporate logos. Its 1951 representation (*below right*), with fangs bared and claws extended, was eventually withdrawn as too aggressive and likely to encourage reckless driving (Jaguar Cars logo; Esso advertisement)

The lion, used as a mark to guarantee a certain standard of silver (*above right*), was also adopted by film moguls Sam Goldwyn and Louis B. Meyer to symbolize MGM and serve as guardian of its quality (*below*). Like the Esso Tiger, it is an aggressive symbol. (Lion hallmark, certifying sterling standard fine silver; MGM trademark)

A 19th-century mosaic of the Seven Deadly Sins (*below left*) chose the cat to represent the sin of anger, and a bloodthirsty cat toying with a mouse (*bottom left*) was employed to great effect by the early women suffragists to publicize the British Government's policy towards hunger strikers. (IRA [anger], from a 19th-century mosaic in Nôtre Dame de Fourvière, Lyon; The Cat and Mouse Act, poster, c. 1914)

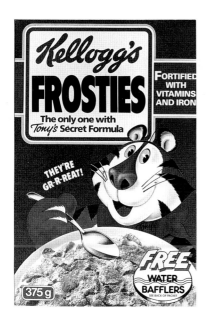

However, anger dispelled and aggression tamed produce singularly appealing images. The obverse of the prowling tiger representing famine (*above right*) is Tony the Tiger (*above*), the friendly creature used by Kellogg's to promote 'Frosties'. A cartoon image obviously aimed at children, it implies that this cereal will impart the strength and vitality of the tiger to all who eat it. A similar message is contained in the beguiling image used by Tate & Lyle to advertise their syrup (*below*), which shows the lion killed by Samson, surrounded by a swarm of bees, and accompanied by the verse from the Book of Judges: 'Out of the strong came forth sweetness.' ('Famine in India', *Punch* cartoon, 1896; advertisement for Kellogg's 'Frosties'; Lyle's Golden Syrup, courtesy Tate & Lyle)

Speed, agility, strength, fierceness — we take from cats, great and small, whatever aspect of their multifarious natures suits our purposes. But whatever characteristic we choose to emphasize, we may be sure that the cat itself will not always conform to expectations (*right*). (Edwin Smith, *Archie the Cat*, 1960s)

Sources

Beadle, M. *The Cat: History, Biology and Behaviour*, London, 1977.

Benson, E.P. (ed.) *The Cult of the Feline*, Washington, 1972.

Bevan, E. *Representations of Animals in Sanctuaries of Artemis and Other Olympian Deities*, Oxford, 1986.

Binford, L. *In Pursuit of the Past*, London, 1983.

Broneer, C. *The Lion Monument at Amphipolis*, Cambridge, Massachusetts, 1941.

Brown, W.L. *The Etruscan Lion*, Oxford, 1960.

Camille, M. *The Gothic Idol*, Cambridge, 1989.

Clutton-Brock, J. *The British Museum Book of Cats*, London, 1988.

de Sélincourt, A. (trs.) *Herodotus, The Histories*, Harmondsworth, 1976.

de Wit, C. *Le Rôle et le sens du lion dans L'Egypte Ancienne*, Leiden, 1951.

Eliade, M. *Shamanism: Archaic Techniques of Ecstasy*, New York, 1964.

Endicott, K. *Batek Negrito Religion*, Oxford, 1979.

Gardner, M. *The Annotated Alice*, Harmondsworth, 1965.

Gettings, F. *The Secret Lore of the Cat*, London, 1989.

Guggisberg, C.A.W. *Simba: The Life of the Lion*, London, 1961.

———*Wild Cats of the World*, New York, 1975.

Harner, M.J. (ed.) *Hallucinogens and Shamanism*, Oxford, 1973.

Langton, N. and B. *The Cat in Ancient Egypt*, Cambridge, 1940.

Laufer, B. *Jade: A Study in Chinese Archaeology and Religion*, New York, 1974.

Lindskog, B. *African Leopard Men*, Uppsala, 1954.

Lipton, M. (ed.) *The Tiger Rugs of Tibet*, London, 1988.

McCall, D.F. 'The Prevalence of Lions: Kings, Deities and Feline Symbolism in Africa and Elsewhere', *Paiduma* 19/20 (1973/4): 130–45.

Mellaart, J. *Earliest Civilizations of the Near East*, London, 1965.

Miller, S.D., and Everett, D.D. *Cats of the World: Biology, Conservation and Management*, Washington, 1986.

Moratto, M.J. *California Archaeology*, London, 1983.

Morris, D. *Catwatching*, London, 1986.

———*Catlore*, London, 1988.

Morrison-Scott, T.C.S. 'The Mummified Cats of Ancient Egypt', in *Proceedings of the Zoological Society of London* 121, no.4 (1952): 861–67.

Mundkur, B. *Cult of the Serpent*, New York, 1983.

Nadelhoffer, H. *Cartier: Jewelers Extraordinary*, London, 1984.

Reichel-Dolmatoff, G. *The Shaman and the Jaguar*, Philadelphia, 1975.

Robicsek, F. *A Study in Maya Art and History: The Mat Symbol*, New York, 1975.

Ruel, M. 'Lions, Leopards and Rulers', *New Society*, 8 January 1970.

Russell, J.B., *A History of Witchcraft: Sorcerers, Heretics and Pagans*, London, 1980.

Saunders, N.J. 'Day of the Jaguar: Rainmaking in a Mexican Village', *Geographical Magazine*, August 1984, pp. 398–405.

———*People of the Jaguar*, London, 1989.

Sayer, A, and Findlay, M. *Encyclopedia of the Cat*, London, 1979.

Serpell, J. *In the Company of Animals*, Oxford, 1986.

Smith, N.J.H. 'Spotted Cats and the Amazon Skin Trade', *Oryx* 13, no.4 (July 1976): 362–71.

Tabor, R. *The Wild Life of the Domestic Cat*, London, 1983.

Thomas, K. *Man and the Natural World: Changing Attitudes in England 1500–1800*. London, 1983.

Toynbee, J.M.C. *Animals in Roman Life and Art*, London, 1973.

Ucko, P.J., and Rosenfeld, A. *Palaeolithic Cave Art*, London, 1967.

Zuidema, R.T. 'The Lion in the City: Royal Symbols of Transition in Cuzco', *Journal of Latin American Lore* 9, no.1 (1983): 39–100.

Acknowledgments

Objects reproduced in the plates, pp.33–64, are in the collections of Bern, Historisches Museum 39; Bologna, Biblioteca Universitaria 37; Cambridge, University Museum of Archaeology 54; London, British Library 56 (MS.4751, f.306); British Museum 38, 45, 51, 52, 63 (on loan); National Gallery 48; Portal Gallery 58; Victoria and Albert Museum 49, 55; Lugano, Thyssen-Bornemisza Collection 64; Manchester, City Art Gallery 44; Modena, Biblioteca Estense (MS. Latino 209, f. 8v) 62; Naples, Museo Archeologico 42–3; New Delhi, C.L. Bharany Collection 36; New York, Metropolitan Museum 46 below; Oxford, Ashmolean Museum 33; Bodleian Library 46; Private Collections 53, 57; Washington, National Museum of Natural History 40.

Sources of photographs and drawings: Ferdinand Anton 41; Associated Press 71 below; P. Clayton 74 centre; Ecole Française d'Archéologie, Athens, 70 below right; W. Forman Archive 33, 37; Salvador Guilliem 67 above right; Marc Henrie A.S.C. 69 below right; Hirmer 76 above; Imperial War Museum 77 below left; International Wild Life Coalition 93 below; V. Kozák, Courtesy American Museum of Natural History, New York, 67 below centre; Emily Lane 94 top left; Mansell-Alinari 75 below; Mimi Lipton 53 below; Museum of London 94 below left; National Army Museum 92 centre; National Film Archive 83 below right; Pitt Rivers Museum, Oxford, 71 top; Réunion des Musées Nationaux 70 top; Leonard Lee Rue III 35; N.J. Saunders 34, 66 below; Pauline Stringfellow 34 top left and bottom left; Edwin Smith 42–3, 68 left, 74 top left, 95 bottom right; Swiss Tourist Office 77 right; Tate and Lyle 95 below left; E. Tweedy 87 below centre; University Museum of Anthropology, Philadelphia 67 below right; R. Wood 74 above right.